A Book of Uncommon Prayer

A Book of Uncommon Prayer

Edited by Theo Dorgan

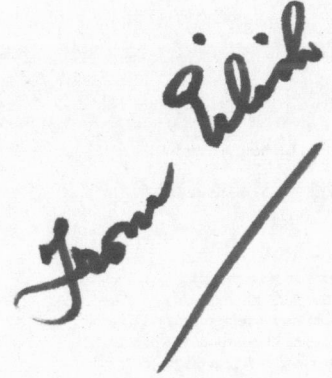

PENGUIN BOOKS

PENGUIN BOOKS

Published by the Penguin Group
Penguin Ireland, 25 St Stephen's Green, Dublin 2, Ireland
(a division of Penguin Books Ltd)
Penguin Books Ltd, 80 Strand, London WC2R 0RL, England
Penguin Group (USA) Inc., 375 Hudson Street, New York, New York 10014, USA
Penguin Group (Australia), 250 Camberwell Road,
Camberwell, Victoria 3124, Australia (a division of Pearson Australia Group Pty Ltd)
Penguin Group (Canada), 90 Eglinton Avenue East, Suite 700, Toronto, Ontario, Canada M4P 2Y3
(a division of Pearson Penguin Canada Inc.)
Penguin Books India Pvt Ltd, 11 Community Centre,
Panchsheel Park, New Delhi – 110 017, India
Penguin Group (NZ), 67 Apollo Drive, Rosedale, North Shore 0632, New Zealand
(a division of Pearson New Zealand Ltd)
Penguin Books (South Africa) (Pty) Ltd, 24 Sturdee Avenue,
Rosebank, Johannesburg 2196, South Africa
Penguin Books Ltd, Registered Offices: 80 Strand, London WC2R 0RL, England

www.penguin.com

First published 2007
1

Collection and introductory matter © Theo Dorgan, 2007

The moral right of the author has been asserted

The acknowledgements on pp. 191–5 constitute an
extension of this copyright page.

Set in Monotype Dante
Typeset by Palimpsest Book Production Limited
Grangemouth, Stirlingshire
Printed in Great Britain by Clays Ltd, St Ives plc

A CIP catalogue record for this book is available from the British Library

ISBN: 978–1–844–88100–0

Contents

Introduction

ɔʒ

Let me record at the outset that I was raised a Catholic, speaking English and Irish, and that my introduction to prayer was also my introduction to the seductive, rhythmic power of the imagination in language. Certain prayers and hymns, especially hymns in English and prayers in Irish, could make the hair stand up on the back of my neck, and so, as I soon discovered, could certain poems and songs. The power of prayer and hymn, I concluded, was the same kind of power as the power of the poem: language deployed with intelligence, flair and feeling. I came to believe in the power and central importance of the word.

At the age of fourteen, easily and without fuss, I discovered that I did not believe in God. I did not believe in God in the same way that I did not believe I could fly unaided, did not believe I could become pregnant, did not believe that by sheer concentration of willpower I could make a malevolent teacher shrivel up and die. I have little interest in arguments for and against the existence of God – such arguments always seem to me somehow futile – but I am interested in prayer because prayer is language under pressure intended to lodge in memory, and I have a lively interest in that.

I want to put these things on record because here before you is a collection of prayers assembled in good faith by a lifelong agnostic.

What I often find off-putting in prayer is its other-directedness, the fact that it is invested in and seeks its warrant from a God who is elsewhere, a reality that transcends our common world. Given the brute and often cruel truths of human existence, extinction not the least of these, it is understandable that some in seeking God seek also to deny or devalue this world in which we live. The idea of a salvific eternity, where one is not poor or powerless, despised or neglected, holds an obvious attraction for the majority of human beings. The negation of pain, the profound comfort of eternal life in the hand of an omnipotent guarantor of all things – these are not negligible promises. But, for believers, it can be all too easy to lose your respect for this fallen world, and when once this bond is loosed it is no step at all to neglectful inattention, and worse. Allowing for the fact that great atrocities have been visited on us by non-believers of one kind or another, nevertheless I am constantly, and I admit naively, shocked by that large cohort of believers who become indifferent to and often actively hostile to this world – as long as they can bask in the assurance of their God that they will be saved in some next world. It is from the ranks of such believers that the suicide bombers come – and the inquisitors, the earth-despoilers, the architects of holocaust. Why is it that so many true believers come to hate this very earth, its substance, its creatures and its people?

It can only be that they do not believe, in any meaningful sense, the central truths of their faiths; they pay lip service to their God, even as they dishonour and traduce the core beliefs they claim that God has taught them. I learned early in life that prayers can be hollow, devoid of meaning, mere empty formulae; I learned early on to listen carefully to the voices of true believers, to see if the bell rang hollow or true. I brought the same test to my selection for this book.

Orthodox or heretical or of some provenance I do not understand or cannot easily categorize, I hope that every text here is a clear, dignified voice speaking memorably, human to human, in the face of the cosmos. I have done what I could to assemble a collection of prayers in which the felt pressures of thought and emotion find an answering sense of life in the language deployed, so that we, reading, are ourselves opened into the direct urgency of human plea or praise. God's certainty is cold and remote; God's dignity must be vast and is surely beyond us: we live on a different scale, we are small things, mortal and often unsure, with intuitions and intimations of a vast unknowable universe. At their best, our prayers enact something unquenchably ambitious in us, the pure desire to speak and to know, to square up to unknowable immensities.

All prayers are composed and spoken by men and women born in a particular place, into a particular tradition. I have chosen texts for this book in large part from the Irish and English traditions because those are the traditions I share, the traditions that are in some sense home to me; it seems to me sensible that, as this book is in some sense a journey, I should set out from the known place. I have of course included many prayers from other traditions, and I have tried in those instances to choose texts that work well in English. Exoticism for the sake of it is a form of disrespect; I hope I have avoided that.

I hope that believers may find here prayers that speak to their living faith. I hope that they will find here words that speak to their unbroken kinship with people of no faith. I hope that non-believers may find here texts that illuminate, however obliquely, the unavoidable question: How should we live, unsustained by belief?

Theo Dorgan

Speaking to God

⁂

It cannot be easy to step outside the bounds of the conventional when addressing God, or gods. As an organized religion gains ground, as its orthodoxies become more and more minutely elaborated, there is less and less room to manoeuvre for that individual who feels pressed by circumstance towards direct speech with the divine. The growth of a priestly caste is chiefly responsible for this: priests have a powerful vested interest in mediating between God and man – and hence a powerful motive for controlling that language and those forms of language in which God is 'properly' addressed. The more elaborate the outward forms and structures of a religion, the more conventional and, eventually, emptied of urgency the prayers of that religion become. It is of course possible for the devout orthodox person to press meaning into a prayer learned by rote, dulled by infinite repetition – the sheer familiarity of words said over and over again can give a comforting sense of belonging, can induce a meditative near-trance which creates a nearness to God.

Borrowing a phrase from Ezekiel, Robert Graves writes of the dictionary as 'a valley of dry bones' and says that the proper business of the poet is to breathe life into these bones, so that they may become articulate, and move about, and dance and caper. The man or woman urgently in need of addressing God directly is also possessed of that need to breathe life into dry bones; the more urgent the impulse, the more lively the language of the resulting prayer is likely to be.

There are as many reasons for speaking to God as there are

ways of so speaking, and I have tried in this section to give as wide a range as possible of speaking, motivated voices. What strikes me most, in these prayers addressed directly to God, is the robust sense of self, and self-worth, displayed by their authors, even when playing the abject. They are addressing, by their own estimations, the lord of all creation, the maker of all things, the master of all that is, was and will be, *and they expect to be heard.* Sometimes the effect borders on the comic, sometimes a small timid phrase will pierce you to the heart, but over and over again, believer or unbeliever, you will find yourself warming to the humanity of these often anonymous authors: they are so alert to circumstance, so full of appetite and busy-ness, so endlessly curious, lustful, remorseful, terrified, elated, in love with the world and aching for peace in the hereafter. They speak to God, *and they expect to be answered.* If I were God, I should be glad to answer them.

2

A riposte to 'God Save the King'.

When wilt thou save the people?
Ebenezer Elliott

When wilt thou save the people?
O God of mercy, when?
The people, Lord, the people,
Not crowns and thrones, but men!
Flowers of thy heart, O God, are they;
Let them not pass like weeds away,
Their heritage a sunless day:
God save the people!

Shall crime bring crime for ever,
Strength aiding still the strong?
Is it thy will, O Father,
That man shall toil for wrong?
'No,' say thy mountains; 'no,' thy skies;
Man's clouded sun shall brightly rise,
And songs be heard instead of sighs;
God save the people!

When wilt thou save the people?
O God of mercy, when?
The people, Lord, the people,
Not crowns and thrones, but men!
God save the people; thine they are
Thy children, as thy angels fair;
From vice, oppression and despair
God save the people!

Black Elk was a holy man of the Oglala Lakota. He was also a baptized Christian, and had little difficulty in reconciling his two religious faiths. In later life he claimed to have met on a number of occasions with the Great Spirit who rules the universe.

Grandfather, Great Spirit
Black Elk, trans. John G. Neihardt

Grandfather, Great Spirit, you have been always, and before you no one has been. There is no other one to pray to but you. You yourself, everything that you see, everything has been made by you. The star nations all over the universe you have finished. The four quarters of the earth you have finished. The day, and in that day, everything you have finished. Grandfather, Great Spirit, lean close to the earth that you may hear the voice I send. You towards where the sun goes down, behold me; Thunder Beings, behold me! You where the White Giant lives in power, behold me! You where the sun shines continually, whence come the day-break star and the day, behold me! You in the depths of the heavens, an eagle of power, behold! And you, Mother Earth, the only Mother, you who have shown mercy to your children!

Hear Me, four quarters of the world – a relative I am! Give me the strength to walk the soft earth, a relative to all that is! Give me the eyes to see and the strength to understand, that I may be like you. With your power only can I face the winds.

Great Spirit, Great Spirit, my Grandfather, all over the earth the faces of living things are all alike. With tenderness have these come up out of the ground. Look upon these faces of children.

Mechtild's visions of the Holy Ghost began when she was twelve and continued all her life. Her vision of hell is sometimes credited with inspiring Dante's depiction of the infernal regions.

O Lord, love me intensely, love me often and long!
Mechtild of Magdeburg, trans. Oliver Davies

O Lord, love me intensely, love me often and long!
For the more often you love me, the purer I become.
The more intensely you love me, the more beautiful I become.
The longer you love me, the holier I become.

An ideal Irish monastery of the tenth century, described by a saint. In another reading, a plea for some kind of absolute communion with his God.

The Wish of Manchán of Liath
trans. Kenneth Hurlstone Jackson

I wish, O son of the Living God, ancient Eternal King, for a secret
    hut in the wilderness that it may be my dwelling.
A very blue shallow well to be beside it, a clear pool for washing
    away sins through the grace of the Holy Ghost.
A beautiful wood close by around it on every side, for the nurture
    of many-voiced birds, to shelter and hide it.
Facing the south for warmth, a little stream across its enclosure, a
    choice ground with abundant bounties which would be good
    for every plant.
A few sage disciples, I will tell their number, humble and obedi-
    ent, to pray to the King.
Four threes, three fours, fit for every need, two sixes in the
    church, both south and north.
Six couples in addition to me myself, praying through the long
    ages to the King who moves the sun.
A lovely church decked with linen, a dwelling for God of Heaven;
    then, bright candles over the holy white Scriptures.
One room to go to for the care of the body, without wantonness,
    without voluptuousness, without meditation of evil.
This is the housekeeping I would undertake, I would choose
    it without concealing; fragrant fresh leeks, hens, speckled
    salmon, bees.
My fill of clothing and of food from the King of good fame, and
    for me to be sitting for a while praying to God in every place.

A ninth-century mathematician and geometer, Alcuin is well described by Siegfried Sassoon: 'Homely and human, numb in feet and fingers, / Alcuin believed in angels . . .'

He lay with quiet heart . . .
Alcuin of York, trans. Helen Waddell

He lay with quiet heart in the stern asleep:
Waking, commanded both the winds and sea.
Christ, though this weary body slumber deep,
Grant that my heart may keep its watch with thee.
O Lamb of God that carried all our sin,
Guard thou my sleep against the enemy.

Author of the Consolation of Philosophy, *the formidably learned Boethius was an important sixth-century translator from the ancient Greek; his Aristotle was a primary text until the twelfth century. Boethius was a vigorous opponent of the Arian heresy; he was executed by Theodoric the Great, who was not.*

O God, whose reason rules the world . . .
Boethius, trans. Michael Counsell

O God, whose reason rules the world,
who formed the starry heights above,
timeless, time's chain far forth you hurled,
unmoved, gave all things power to move.
Prevailed on by no outside cause
to fashion all reality;
ideas of love and mental laws
moulded the noble world we see.
Your nature perfect beauty, thus
you made the world in tenderness
with sights and sounds to conjure us
to love the source of loveliness.
You named the primal elements,
of earth and water, air and fire,
and balanced out their influence
that none might lower be or higher.
O Father, give me power to climb
and wash in fountains filled with light,
weighed down no more by things of time,
lit by your shining in the night.
The sight of you begins our day,

with you its evening we shall spend;
you carry us, and lead the way,
the journey, and the journey's end.

An example of the way in which missionary work in Africa found expression in artless prayer.

Ghanaian Christian Prayer

The sun has disappeared,
I have switched off the light,
and my wife and children are asleep.
The animals in the forest are full of fear,
and so are the people on their mats.
They prefer the day with your sun to the night
but I still know that your moon is there,
and your eyes and also your hands.
Thus I am not afraid.
This day again you led us wonderfully.
Everybody went to his mat satisfied and full.
Renew us during our sleep,
that in the morning we may come afresh to our daily jobs.
Be with our brothers far away in Asia
who may be getting up now. Amen.

Nerving oneself to go on a journey is a common theme of early Irish prayers. In this prayer the parallels between the dangers of the spiritual journey and those of the known world are drawn with a marked deftness by someone who clearly loved horses.

The First Word I Say

The first word I say
In the morning, when I arise:
May Christ's cross be my armour about me.

I shall put on the Lord's protection today.
A sneeze I hear,
It is not my God; I will not believe in it.

I shall arm myself splendidly,
And not believe any superstition, for it is not right.
He who created me shall give me strength.

My mind is set on a journey,
My intent is to put to sea.
A beneficial plan, a gift it will be.

My mind is set on a plan,
My intent is to put to sea,
A beneficial plan, O Lord, it will be.

A crow shall raise its wing,
Intending to go far.
A beneficial plan, it will be better.

A crow shall raise its wing,
Intending to go to Rome.
A beneficial plan, it will be fine.

Saddle the bay with white nostrils,
Eager to run, with a rough coat.
King of Heaven, we would need God's aid.

Saddle the short-haired bay,
With easy gait and ambling pace.
Where there is a nose, there will be a sneeze!

Saddle the bay with the long leap,
With easy gait and keen pace.
An unlucky sneeze shall not check the brave.

Earth's company is burdensome, and thick the briar's leaves,
Bitter the drinking horn of sweet mead.
Lord of Heaven, smooth the way of my journey.

O royal offspring, victorious Redeemer,
Peter, head of every nation,
St Brigid, bless our journey.

Aseneth, rejecting the false idol for the true God, dramatizes and seals the integrity of her conversion by repudiating her birth father, the priest Pentephres. Joseph and Aseneth, *the text from which this comes, is likely one of the large number of Second Temple period prayers of petition.*

from Prayer of a Convert to Judaism
trans. Randall D. Chesnutt

Lord, God of the ages,
who created all things and brought them to life,
who gave the breath of life to all your creation,
who brought the invisible things out into the light,
who made the things which exist and which appear out of those
    which do not appear and do not exist,
who raised up the heaven and laid its foundation on a dome upon
    the back of the winds,
who laid the earth's foundation upon the waters,
who placed great stones upon the watery abyss.
And the stones will not sink
but are like oak leaves on top of the waters,
and they are living stones,
and they hear your voice, Lord,
and they keep your commandments which you commanded
    them,
and from your ordinances they do not deviate
but do your will to the end.
For you, Lord, spoke and they were alive,
from your word, Lord, is life for all your creatures.
To you I come for refuge, Lord,
and to you I will cry out, Lord,
to you I will pour out my plea,

to you I will confess my sins,

and to you I will reveal my transgressions.

Spare me, Lord,

for I have sinned often in your sight.

I have transgressed and committed sacrilege,

and I have spoken evil and unspeakable things in your sight.

My mouth is defiled from sacrifices to idols

and from the table of the gods of the Egyptians.

I have sinned, Lord,

in your sight I have sinned often in ignorance,

and I have worshipped dead and deaf idols.

And now I am not worthy to open my mouth to you, Lord.

And I, Aseneth, daughter of Pentephres the priest,

the virgin and princess,

who was at one time pompous and arrogant

and thriving in my riches beyond all people,

am now an orphan and desolate and forsaken by all people.

To you I come for refuge, Lord,

and to you I bring my plea,

and to you I will cry out.

Rescue me before I am seized by those who pursue me.

For as a frightened little child flees to his father,

and the father stretches out his hands and picks him up from the
    ground

and embraces him against his breast,

and the child clutches his hands tightly around his father's neck

and recovers from his fear

and rests against his father's breast,

while the father smiles at his childish confusion,

so you also, Lord, stretch out your hands to me as does a father
    who loves his child,

and pick me up from the ground.
For behold, the wily old lion pursues me,
because he is the father of the Egyptians' gods,
and his children are the gods of the frenzied idolaters.
And I have come to hate them,
for they are the lion's children,
and I threw them all away from me and destroyed them.
And their father the lion pursues me ferociously.
But you, Lord, rescue me from his hands,
and from his mouth remove me,
lest he snatch me away like a lion
and tear me to pieces,
and throw me into the flame of fire,
and the fire will throw me into the storm,
and the storm will envelop me in darkness
and throw me out into the depths of the sea,
and the great eternal sea monster will consume me,
and I will perish eternally.
Rescue me, Lord, before all these things come upon me.
Rescue me, Lord, the desolate and isolated one,
because my father and mother have disowned me and said,
'Aseneth is not our daughter',
because I destroyed and shattered their gods
and came to hate them.
And now I am an orphan and desolate,
and I have no other hope except in you, Lord,
and no other refuge besides your mercy, Lord,
because you are the father of orphans
and a protector of the persecuted
and a helper of the oppressed.
Have mercy on me, Lord, and keep watch over me,

the chaste virgin who is forsaken and an orphan,
because you, Lord, are a sweet and good and gentle father.
Whose father is as sweet as you, Lord?
And which one is as quick in mercy as you, Lord?
For behold, all the gifts of my father, Pentephres,
which he has given to me for an inheritance are temporary and
   vanishing,
but the gifts of your inheritance, Lord, are imperishable and
   eternal.

The Watchers were a race of divine beings, 'those who watch' or 'those who are awake'. These Watchers feature in the Book of Enoch and the Book of Jubilees. Enoch has it that, 'While they are on earth, they teach women about charms, spells, root-cutting, and plants and various other arts including astrology.'

Jubilees 10: 3–6
trans. John Endres

3   [Noah] prayed in the presence of God his Lord and said: 'Lord of the spirits which are in all flesh, You, who have shown me mercy and saved me and my sons from the waters of the Flood and did not make me perish (as You did to the children of destruction) since Your kindness to me has been great, and great has been your mercy to my soul.

May Your kindness be raised high over Your children's children, and may the evil spirits not rule over them lest they destroy them from the earth.

4   Now bless me and my sons so we might increase and grow numerous and fill the earth.

5   And You know how your Watchers acted – the fathers of these spirits – during my days.

Now these spirits who are still alive – lock them up and keep them captive in the place of judgement, so they may not cause corruption among the children of Your servant, my Lord, since they are vicious and were created for corrupting.

6   Do not let them rule over the spirits of the living since You alone know their judgement.

Let them have no power over the children of the just from now on and for evermore.'

Astley was commander of the Royalist infantry at the Battle of Edgehill in 1642, before which he is said to have composed this prayer. He was indeed busy.

On the Eve of Battle
General Lord Astley

O Lord, thou knowest how busy I must be this day;
if I forget thee, do not thou forget me: for Christ's sake.

Traditional Breton fisherman's prayer. Until recent times, it was a fact that one in six of Bretons who made their living from the sea were destined to drown.

The Boat So Small

Look after me, dear Lord:
my boat is so small,
and your ocean is so vast.

The hermit, in all traditions, is prone to the tortures of distraction. This early Irish monk wittily rehearses his temptations, not without some admiration for their ingenious energy.

On the Flightiness of Thought

Shame on my thoughts, how they stray from me! I fear great danger from this on the Day of Eternal Judgement.

During the psalms they wander on a path that is not right: they run, they distract, they misbehave before the eyes of the great God.

Through eager assemblies, through companies of lewd women, through woods, through cities, – swifter they are than the wind.

One moment they follow ways of loveliness, and the next ways of riotous shame – no lie!

Without a ferry or a false step they cross every sea: swiftly they leap in one bound from earth to heaven.

They run – not a course of great wisdom – near, far: following paths of great foolishness they reach their home.

Though one should try to bind them or put shackles on their feet, they are neither constant nor inclined to rest a while.

Neither the edge of a sword nor the stripe of lash will subdue them: slippery as an eel's tail they elude my grasp.

Neither lock nor well-constructed dungeon, nor any fetter on earth, neither stronghold nor sea nor bleak fastness restrains them from their course.

O beloved, truly chaste Christ, to whom every eye is clear, may the grace of the sevenfold spirit come to keep them, to hold them in check!

Rule this heart of mine, O swift God of the elements, that you may be my love, and that I may do your will!

That I may reach Christ with his chosen companions, that we may be together: they are neither fickle nor inconstant – they are not as I am.

Considering that Islam enjoins the believer to fear hell and hope for paradise, as of course do other religions, it is unusual to find a prayer that addresses God in these terms.

Old Muslim Prayer

O Lord!
If I worship You from fear of hell,
let me burn in hell;
if I worship you hoping for Paradise,
exclude me from Paradise;
but if I worship You for Your own sake only,
do not withhold from me Your Eternal Beauty.

Carman, a Canadian poet, died in 1929.

Veni Creator

Bliss Carman

I

Lord of the grass and hill,
Lord of the rain,
White Overlord of will,
Master of pain,

I who am dust and air
Blown through the halls of death,
Like a pale ghost of prayer –
I am thy breath.

Lord of the blade and leaf,
Lord of the bloom,
Sheer Overlord of grief,
Master of doom,

Lonely as wind or snow,
Through the vague world and dim,
Vagrant and glad I go;
I am thy whim.

Lord of the storm and lull,
Lord of the sea,
I am thy broken gull,
Blown far alee.

Lord of the harvest dew,
Lord of the dawn,
Star of the paling blue
Darkling and gone,

Lost on the mountain height
Where the first winds are stirred,
Out of the wells of night
I am thy word.

Lord of the haunted hush,
Where raptures throng,
I am thy hermit thrush,
Ending no song.

Lord of the frost and cold,
Lord of the North,
When the red sun grows old
And day goes forth,

I shall put off this girth –
Go glad and free,
Earth to my mother earth,
Spirit to thee.

II

Lord of my heart's elation,
Spirit of things unseen,
Be thou my aspiration
Consuming and serene!

Bear up, bear out, bear onward
This mortal soul alone,
To selfhood or oblivion,
Incredibly thine own –

As the foamheads are loosened
And blown along the sea,
Or sink and merge forever
In that which bids them be.

I, too, must climb in wonder,
Uplift at thy command –
Be one with my frail fellow
Beneath the wind's strong hand,

A fleet and shadowy column
Of dust or mountain rain,
To walk the earth a moment
And be dissolved again.

Be thou my exaltation
Or fortitude of mien,
Lord of the world's elation
Thou breath of things unseen!

The lighting of a particularly large candle in Christian churches at Easter-time is a custom of great antiquity. It evokes for some the Zoroastrian conception of God as the bringer of fire and light, for others the special place given to fire and light in the Greek tradition.

Hymn at the Lighting of the Paschal Candle
Irish

Fiery Creator of fire,
Light Giver of light,
Life and Author of life,
Salvation and Bestower of salvation,
In case the lamps should abandon
The joys of this night,
You who do not desire our death
Give light to our breast.

To those wandering from Egypt,
You bestow the double grace,
You show the veil of cloud,
And give the nocturnal light.
With a pillar of cloud in the day,
You protect the people as they go,
With a pillar of fire at evening,
You dispel the night with light.

You call out to your servant from the flame,
You do not spurn the bush of thorns,
And though you are consuming fire,
You do not burn what you illumine.
Now it is time that the cloudy bee-bread

Should be consumed, all impurity boiled away,
And the waxen flesh should shine
With the glow of the Holy Spirit.

You store now in the recesses of the comb
The sweet food of the divine honey,
And purifying the inmost cells of the heart,
You have filled them with your word;
That the swarm of the new brood,
Chosen by your mouth and spirit,
May leave their burdens and win heaven
On wings now free from care.

An extraordinary campaigner for human rights in all fields, Sojourner Truth (a name she adopted when she began to preach) was born in 1797 and died in 1883; she began life as a slave and ended it a genuine American heroine. This text is everywhere attributed to her, but nobody seems able to source it.

A Question
attrib. to Sojourner Truth

Dear God, if the first woman you ever made was strong enough to turn the whole world upside down, all alone, ought not women together be able to turn it rightside up again?

May the Stubble and the Grass Praise You
Irish (tenth or eleventh century)

May the stubble and the grass praise you,
Aaron and Moses praised you,
May the seven days and the stars praise you,
May male and female praise you,
May the lower and upper air praise you,
May books and letters praise you,
May the fish in the river praise you,
May thought and action praise you,
May the sand and the earth praise you,
May all the good things created praise you,
And I too shall praise you, Lord of Glory,
Hail to you, glorious Lord!

Deliver Us
Teresa of Ávila

God, deliver us from sullen saints!

The great prophet of democracy, which he celebrated in near-religious terms, Whitman had a profound sense of the godly in the common man, of the divine beauty in common things.

God
Walt Whitman

Why should I wish to see You better than this day? I see some-
    thing
of You in each hour of the twenty-four, and each moment then;
In the faces of men and women I see You, and in my own face in
    the glass.
I find letters from You dropped in the street, and every one is
    signed by Your name.

And I leave them where they are, for I know that wheresoe'er I go
Others will punctually come for ever and ever.

Reportedly translated from a sixteenth-century original.

An Aztec Prayer

Lord most giving and resourceful, I implore you: make it your will that this people enjoy the goods and riches you naturally give, that naturally issue from you, that are pleasing and savoury, that delight and comfort, though lasting but briefly, passing away as if in a dream.

Oh Allah!
Prophet Mohammed

Oh Allah!
I consult You as You are all Knowing,
and I seek ability from Your power
and I ask You for Your great favour,
For You have power
but I do not,
and You have knowledge
but I do not,
and You know all hidden matters.

Oh Allah!
If You know that this matter is good for me in my religion,
my livelihood and my life in the Hereafter,
then make it easy and bless it;
and if You know that this matter is evil for me in my religion,
my livelihood and my life in the Hereafter,
then keep it away from me and keep me away from it,
and choose what is good for me wherever it is,
and make me pleased with it.

The Navigatio Sancti Brendani Abbatis *was a hugely influential religious teaching text, whether or not it is an account of a real voyage. Brendan's great theme was the soul's dilemma, torn between earth and heaven.*

Shall I abandon, O King of mysteries . . .
'A pilgrim's plea', attrib. to St Brendan, trans. Robert van de Weyer

Shall I abandon, O King of mysteries, the soft comforts of home?
Shall I turn my back on my native land, and my face towards the sea?

Shall I put myself wholly at your mercy,
without silver, without a horse,
without fame and honour?
Shall I throw myself wholly on you,
without sword and shield, without food and drink,
without a bed to lie on?
Shall I say farewell to my beautiful land, placing myself under your
    yoke?

Shall I pour out my heart to you, confessing my manifold sins and
    begging forgiveness,
tears streaming down my cheeks?
Shall I leave the prints of my knees on the sandy beach,
a record of my final prayer in my native land?

Shall I then suffer every kind of wound that the sea can inflict?
Shall I then take my tiny currach across the wide sparkling ocean?
O King of the glorious heaven, shall I go of my own choice upon
    the sea?
O Christ, will you help me on the wild waves?

Kierkegaard believed that the turbulence of radical freedom could lead only to despair. Peace, spiritual peace, eluded him all his life.

For Inward Peace
Søren Kierkegaard

Dear God make calm the waves in this heart, make still that storm.
Be calm, my soul, that God may rest in you,
God's peace wash over you.
Dear God you grant us peace, peace that the whole world
cannot wash away.

It might be thought blasphemous that one should presume (outside revelation) to give a voice to God, but a surprising number of people have done so. Hellenistic literature is full of plays, for instance, where the gods are heard to speak, and this does not seem to have unduly worried anybody, but one may be reasonably sure that the authors did not expect their audiences literally to believe a god stood speaking on the stage. In the monotheistic religions, equally, speaker and listener (or author and reader) agree in the normal way to listen or read as if it is God speaking, not so much with belief as with a willing suspension of disbelief. I give instances of this in the following pages, but I am not so sure that the author, or authors, of the Essene Gospel of Peace do not in some sense wish us to read as if reading the authentic voice of God; for that matter, Michael Hartnett in his sonnet here seems on the verge of himself believing that he is giving voice to some real other.

The next prayer is from the Carmina Gadelica, or Charms of the Gaels, a collection of Gaelic prayers and hymns collected and translated at the end of the nineteenth century in the Highlands and Western Isles of Scotland by the extraordinary Alexander Carmichael.

The Gift of Power

I am the gift, I am the Poor,
I am the Man of this night.

I am the Son of God in the door,
On Monday seeking the gifts.

Noble is Bride the gentle fair on her knee,
Noble the King of glory on her breast.

Son of the moon, Son of the sun,
Great Son of Mary of God-like mind.

A cross on each right shoulder,
I am in the door, open thou.

I see the hills, I see the strand,
I see angels heralding on high.

I see the dove, shapely, benign,
Coming with kindness and friendship to us.

Weekes was a Dublin Theosophist, acquaintance of Yeats and George Russell.

That
Charles Weekes

What is that beyond thy life,
And beyond all life around,
Which, when thy quick brain is still,
Nods to thee from the stars?
Lo, it says, thou hast found
Me, the lonely, lonely one.

In 1928 Edmond Bordeaux Szekely first published his translation of the Essene Gospel of Peace. The English version appeared in 1937, a fragment of the complete manuscript which exists in Aramaic in the Secret Archives of the Vatican. Spurred by his friend Aldous Huxley to produce a more readable translation, Szekely published a new version in 1981; this prayer is taken from Book 2.

God Speaks to Man
trans. Edmond Bordeaux Szekely

> I speak to you.
> Be still
> Know I am God.
>
> I spoke to you when you were born.
> Be still
> Know I am God.
>
> I spoke to you at your first sight.
> Be still
> Know I am God.
>
> I spoke to you at your first word.
> Be still
> Know I am God.
>
> I spoke to you at your first thought.
> Be still
> Know I am God.

I spoke to you at your first love.
Be still
Know I am God.

I spoke to you at your first song.
Be still
Know I am God.

I speak to you through the grass of the meadows.
Be still
Know I am God.

I speak to you through the trees of the forests.
Be still
Know I am God.

I speak to you through the valleys and the hills.
Be still
Know I am God.

I speak to you through the Holy Mountains.
Be still
Know I am God.

I speak to you through the rain and snow.
Be still
Know I am God.

I speak to you through the waves of the sea.
Be still
Know I am God.

I speak to you through the dew of the morning.
Be still
Know I am God.

I speak to you through the peace of the evening.
Be still
Know I am God.

I speak to you through the splendour of the sun.
Be still
Know I am God.

I speak to you through the brilliant stars.
Be still
Know I am God.

I speak to you through the storm and the clouds.
Be still
Know I am God.

I speak to you through the thunder and lightning.
Be still
Know I am God.

I speak to you through the mysterious rainbow.
Be still
Know I am God.

I will speak to you when you are alone.
Be still
Know I am God.

I will speak to you through the Wisdom of the Ancients.
Be still
Know I am God.

I will speak to you at the end of time.
Be still
Know I am God.

I will speak to you when you have seen my Angels.
Be still
Know I am God.

I will speak to you throughout Eternity.
Be still
Know I am God.

I speak to you.
Be still
Know I am God.

Hartnett's imagination ranged freely in time and space, at home in this and other worlds like no other poet of our time. He was beyond uncanny.

Thirteen Sonnets, 1
Michael Hartnett

I have been stone, dust of space, sea and sphere:
flamed in the supernova before man
or manmade gods made claim to have shaped me.
I have always been, will always be, I
am a pinch of earth compressed in the span
of a snail-shell: galaxies' energy,
the centre of the sun, the arch of sky.
I became all that all things ever can.
I *will* be here: I have always been here.
Buddha had to walk upon me: my snows
were not so kind, my ice was sharp as grass.
Upon me, even Christ encountered fear:
the nails were mine, the mallet mine, the blows
were mine. *I* grew the tree that grew the Cross.

Gratitude

☙

We do not, as a rule, enjoy feeling grateful or thankful, or at least not for very long. Gratitude is often a passive state, a condition or emotion bordering on the helpless, which then slides away into a kind of resentment. Even in cultures that do not favour the ego as much as our present Western culture does, gratitude is a problem for many. To be grateful is to be the recipient, and receiving implies a giver – towards whom one incurs an obligation. Buddhist societies seem to be better at handling simple gratitude, as what is given is simply a manifestation of what is; there is no implied giver and hence no threat to the ego. In God-centred religions there is a primary giver, the Lord of creation, and while one may be grateful for what the Lord gives, one is made conscious by that very gratitude of being inferior to the giver. This difficulty with gratitude is one of the more puzzling examples of human psychology at war with an individual's professed beliefs: how often do people really mean it, for instance, when they give thanks to God for – well, anything? How many people, waking to pain or dread or simply to the return of daily boredom, experience a sense of gratitude for that small miracle of returning to consciousness, of not being dead yet? Gratitude as a passive feeling is an evanescent thing, a fleeting emotion.

Active gratitude, the appreciation of *and* inclination to return kindness, is a phenomenon of a different order. Gratitude of this kind arises from an unthreatened sense of the authorship of order, of how things are arranged (and by whom or what); it accepts the amplified emotion that accompanies the insight and moves immediately to the *expression* of gratitude. We *give* thanks. Appreciation is coupled with the impulse to return; there is, in gratitude of this kind, a heightened consciousness which experiences in the state of gratitude a simultaneous impulse to transfer or transform this experience by doing, by giving or at the very least by acknowledging. This impulse can be the outcome of thought, or it can be purely instinctive – think of Coleridge's Mariner who 'blessed them unaware' – but it carries with it the aftershock of the transmission of grace, the steadying of self that comes with the flow of onwardness.

The prayers in this section are founded in this sense of active gratitude, but they are borne up on a wider sea of what we might call wonder. The very act of prayer is an expression of wonder, most fundamentally wonder at the given. Some prayers indeed interrogate and acknowledge the God or god behind the given, while others register simply an urge to give thanks for what is given. Some move from gratitude for the phenomenal world to giving thanks to its creator, however conceived; others express in rhapsodic terms delight in and awe at the enduring miracle of this world, this life.

ᘒ

This verse was written down by an eleventh-century scribe, but appears to date from the ninth century.

The Lord of Creation
trans. Gerard Murphy

Let us adore the Lord,
maker of wondrous works,
great bright Heaven with its angels,
the white-waved sea on earth.

Elizabeth Staeglin was one of the authors of the Nonnenbuch, *the* Nuns' Book, *of the medieval monastery of Töss, at Winterthur in Switzerland.*

Uplifted in God
Elizabeth Staeglin of Töss, trans. Brian Pickett

Praise God!
I have been shown, as far as can be,
what God is and where God is . . .

Wonder of all!
I swim in the Godhead
like an eagle in the air.

Prayer for the Great Family
Gary Snyder

Gratitude to Mother Earth, sailing through night and day –
    and to her soil, rich, rare, and sweet
        in our minds so be it.

Gratitude to Plants, the sun-facing light-changing leaf
        and fine root-hairs, standing still through wind
        and rain, their dance is in the flowing spiral grain
        in our minds so be it.

Gratitude to Air, bearing the soaring Swift and the silent
        Owl at dawn. Breath of our song
    clear spirit breeze
        in our minds so be it.

Gratitude to Wild Beings, our brothers, teaching secrets,
        freedoms, and ways, who share with us their milk,
        self-complete, brave, and aware
        in our minds so be it.

Gratitude to Water, clouds, lakes, rivers, glaciers,
        holding or releasing, streaming through all
    our bodies salty seas
        in our minds so be it.

Gratitude to the Sun, blinding pulsing light through
        trunks of trees, through mists, warming caves where
        bears and snakes sleep – he who wakes us –
        in our minds so be it.

Gratitude to the Great Sky
> who holds billions of stars – and goes yet beyond that –
> beyond all powers, and thoughts,
> and yet is within us –
> Grandfather Space
> The Mind is his Wife

> so be it.

God with Me Lying Down
from the Carmina Gadelica

God with me lying down,
God with me rising up,
God with me in each ray of light,
Nor I a ray of joy without Him,
Nor one ray without Him.

Christ with me sleeping,
Christ with me waking,
Christ with me watching,
Every day and night,
Each day and night.

God with me protecting,
The Lord with me directing,
The Spirit with me strengthening,
For ever and for evermore,
Ever and evermore, Amen.
Chief of chiefs, Amen.

Precentor of the Abbey of Rievaulx in the late twelfth century, Matthew was a prolific writer, especially of letters, and busied himself extensively in ecclesiastical and political affairs.

The winter will lose its cold . . .
Matthew of Rievaulx

The winter will lose its cold,
as the snow will be without whiteness,
the night without darkness,
the heavens without stars,
the day without light.
The flower will lose its beauty,
all fountains their water,
the sea its fish,
the tree its birds,
the forest its beasts,
the earth its harvest –
All these things will pass before
anyone breaks the bonds of our love,
and before I cease caring for you in my heart.
May your days be happy in number as flakes of snow,
may your nights be peaceful,
and may you be without troubles.

From The Harp Book of Graces, *published by Harp Lager in 1967.*
Given this provenance, one may raise an eyebrow at the attribution of the
first of these to Jonathan Swift.

Sardonic Graces

1 *attributed to Dean Swift*

For rabbits young and rabbits old
For rabbits hot and rabbits cold,
For rabbits tender, rabbits tough,
We thank Thee, Lord: we've had enough.

2 *Hodge's Grace*

Heavenly Father, bless us,
And keep us all alive;
There's ten of us to dinner
And not enough for five.

The Invocation of the Graces
from the Carmina Gadelica

I bathe thy palms
In showers of wine,
In the lustral fire,
In the seven elements,
In the juice of the rasps,
In the milk of honey,
And I place the nine pure choice graces
In thy fair fond face,

The grace of form,
The grace of voice,
The grace of fortune,
The grace of goodness,
The grace of wisdom,
The grace of charity,
The grace of choice maidenliness,
The grace of whole-souled loveliness,
The grace of goodly speech.

Dark is yonder town,
Dark are those therein,
Thou art the brown swan,
Going in among them.
Their hearts are under thy control,
Their tongues are beneath thy sole,
Nor will they ever utter a word
To give thee offence.

A shade art thou in the heat,
A shelter art thou in the cold,
Eyes art thou to the blind,
A staff art thou to the pilgrim,
An island art thou at sea,
A fortress art thou on land,
A well art thou in the desert,
Health art thou to the ailing.

Thine is the skill of the Fairy Woman,
Thine is the virtue of Bride the calm,
Thine is the faith of Mary the mild,
Thine is the tact of the woman of Greece,
Thine is the beauty of Emir the lovely,
Thine is the tenderness of Darthula delightful,
Thine is the courage of Maedbh the strong,
Thine is the charm of Binne-bheul.

Thou art the joy of all joyous things,
Thou art the light of the beam of the sun,
Thou art the door of the chief of hospitality,
Thou art the surpassing star of guidance,
Thou art the step of the deer of the hill,
Thou art the step of the steed of the plain,
Thou art the grace of the swan of swimming,
Thou art the loveliness of all lovely desires.

The lovely likeness of the Lord
Is in thy pure face,
The loveliest likeness that
Was upon earth.

The best hour of the day be thine,
The best day of the week be thine,
The best week of the year be thine,
The best year in the Son of God's domain be thine.

Peter has come and Paul has come,
James has come and John has come,
Muriel and Mary Virgin have come,
Uriel the all-beneficent has come,
Ariel the beauteousness of the young has come,
Gabriel the seer of the Virgin has come,
Raphael the prince of the valiant has come,
And Michael the chief of the hosts has come,
And Jesus Christ the mild has come,
And the Spirit of true guidance has come,
And the King of kings has come on the helm,
To bestow on thee their affection and their love,
To bestow on thee their affection and their love.

MacDiarmid was a tempestuous, controversial genius, the towering figure in twentieth-century Scottish poetry, a polemical communist and visionary.

A Moment in Eternity I
Hugh MacDiarmid

. . . I shone within my thoughts
As God within us shines.

And the wind came,
Multitudinous and light
I whirled in exultations inexpressible
– An unpicturable, clear,
Soaring and glorying,
Swift consciousness,
A cosmos turning like a song of spheres
On apices of praise,
A separate colour,
An essential element and conscious part
Of successive and stupendous dreams
In God's own heart!

And the wind ceased
And like a light I stood,
A flame of glorious and complex resolve,
Within God's heart.
I knew then that a new tree,
A new tree and a strange,
Stood beautifully in Heaven.
I knew that a new light

Stood in God's heart
And a light unlike
The Twice Ten Thousand Lights
That stood there,
Shining equally with me,
And giving and receiving increase of light
Like the flame that I was
Perpetually.
And I knew that when the wind rose
This new tree would stand still
Multiplied in light but motionless.

And I knew that when God dreamt
And His creative impulses
Ran through us like a wind
And we flew like clear and coloured
Flames in His dreams
(Adorations, Gratitudes and Joys
Plenary and boon and pure,
Crystal and burning-gold and scarlet
Competing and co-operating flames
Reflecting His desires,
Flashing like epical imaginings
And burning virgin steeps
With ceaseless swift apotheoses)
One light would stand unmoved . . .

Dickinson was brought up in a puritan, not to say Puritan, town, was influenced by the Metaphysicals and was a frequent reader of the Book of Revelations.

Exultation
Emily Dickinson

Exultation is the going
Of an inland soul to sea,
Past the houses – past the headlands –
Into deep Eternity.

Bred as we, among the mountains,
Can the sailor understand

The divine intoxication
Of the first league out from land?

Hopkins was a Jesuit priest and a poet, balanced between a near-breathless nature mysticism and impeccable orthodoxy.

God's Grandeur
Gerard Manley Hopkins

The world is charged with the grandeur of God,
It will flame out, like shining from shook foil,
It gathers to a greatness like the ooze of oil
Crushed. Why do men then now not reck His rod?
Generations have trod, have trod, have trod;
And all is smeared with trade; bleared, smeared with toil;
And bears man's smudge, and shares man's smell; the soil
Is bare now, nor can foot feel being shod.
And for all this, nature is never spent;
There lives the dearest freshness deep down things;
And though the last lights from the black west went,
Oh, morning at the brown brink eastwards springs –
Because the Holy Ghost over the bent
World broods with warm breast and with, ah, bright wings.

God's World
Edna St Vincent Millay

O world, I cannot hold thee close enough!
   Thy winds, thy wide grey skies!
   Thy mists, that roll and rise!
Thy woods, this autumn day, that ache and sag
And all but cry with colour! That gaunt crag
To crush! To lift the lean of that black bluff!
World, World, I cannot get thee close enough!

Long have I known a glory in it all,
   But never knew I this;
   Here such a passion is
As stretcheth me apart, – Lord, I do fear
Thou'st made the world too beautiful this year;
My soul is all but out of me, – let fall
No burning leaf; prithee, let no bird call.

Hesiod has been described by the scholar M. L. West as 'a surly, conservative countryman, given to reflection . . . who felt the gods' presence heavy about him'. The Theogony *is a synthesis of Greek narratives of the gods, a first ordering of that pantheon.*

from Theogony
Hesiod, trans. Hugh G. Evelyn-White

Hail! Children of Zeus! Grant lovely song and celebrate the holy
    race of the deathless gods who are for ever,
those that were born of Earth and starry Heaven and gloomy
    Night
and them that briny Sea did rear. Tell how at the first gods and
earth came to be, and rivers, and the boundless sea with its
raging swell, and the gleaming stars, and the wide heaven above,
and the gods who were born of them, givers of good things, and
how they divided their wealth, and how they shared their
    honours
amongst them, and also how at the first they took many-folded
    Olympus. These things declare to me from the beginning, ye
    Muses
who dwell in the house of Olympus, and tell me which of them
first came to be.

How Admirable the Earth
Walt Whitman

How admirable
the cool-breathed earth!
Earth of the slumbering liquid trees!
Earth of departed sunsets!
Earth of the mountains!
Earth of the full moon tinged with blue!
Earth of the limpid grey of clouds!
Far-swooping, elbow'd earth!
Rich apple-blossomed earth!
How reverence-waking
the voluptuous earth!

All You Big Things, Bless the Lord

All you *big* things, bless the Lord
Mount Kilimanjaro and Lake Victoria
The Rift Valley and the Serengeti Plain
Fat baboabs and shady mango trees
All eucalyptus and tamarind trees
Bless the Lord
Praise and extol Him for ever and ever.

All you tiny things, bless the Lord
Busy black ants and hopping fleas
Wriggling tadpoles and mosquito larvae
Flying locusts and water drops
Pollen dust and tsetse flies
Millet seeds and dried dagaa
Bless the Lord,
Praise and extol Him for ever and ever.

Spells, Charms and Oracles

❧

Spells and charms are the direct speech of the body. They presume on the part of the speaker or singer a direct connection between the self in its body and the great weight of a powerful and mysterious universe. There is an intuition of the truth that all things are connected, a belief economically expressed in the Sanskrit phrase 'Tat tvam asi' – 'That thou art.' The universe exists as a field of power sustaining all individual instances or articulations of power, so that it is possible, for instance, for the hunter to connect with his prey by travelling known or intuited pathways of power to reach out and touch it at a distance, collapsing time and space. Every charm or spell is a bid for power.

Charms and spells come down to us as both individual and communal speech. I see and hear some sailor invoking protection on his journey, and I do the same, and two who observe us follow suit, and now four follow us, then eight, until the prayer or charm or gesture has spread far and irrevocably beyond us. The leap from individual gesture to social articulation of that gesture is an amazingly rapid process, a form of contagion that gains a deep and wide currency.

If the charm or spell is a bid for power, it is also implicitly an alignment with greater powers. Unlike most other forms of prayer, spells and charms lay a heavy emphasis on correspondence, on likeness and similitude, on 'as above, so below'. They tend towards the concrete rather than the universal, towards utterance based on direct observation rather than rehearsed speech that articulates a codified belief system mediated through authority.

The 'Journey Charm' in this chapter allows us a rare glimpse of the passing over from the mythopoeic (or what is sometimes called pagan or animistic) towards the restraint of power inside an explanatory system – in this case, Christianity – but there are many contemporary instances (see, for instance, Diana O'Hehir's 'Spell for Protecting the Heart after Death' in this chapter) of the impulse to power speaking directly in the here-and-now.

The oracle occupies an ambiguous position somewhere between the shamanic voice of power and the ruthlessness of organized cosmology and religion. An oracle is an utterance offering spiritual guidance; the word can also mean the medium who pronounces the oracle, but I use it here in the former sense. I have included a few of the Sibylline Oracles here. Heraclitus tells us that the Sibyl's is an ancient voice, perhaps thousands of years old. Originally a crone with access to the wisdom of the ancients, speaking prophetically to her supplicant visitors, the Sibyl eventually becomes a voice of mystery whose oracles are understood only when interpreted by a coterie of priests. Inevitably, the desire to perpetuate and extend the privileges accruing to the priestly caste and its world view acts in time not only to block the direct dialogue with power, but also in effect to negate the dialogue, to strip out the possibility of direct communication.

This is why oracles, and the powers of oracles, are fated to decay. Charms, spells and invocations, however, we seem to have with us always.

ↅ

Many religions number the names of God; in the Qur'an, for instance, Allah is said to have ninety-nine names. The names are most often in the form of attributes.

God is hidden . . .

God is hidden, no man knoweth his form,
No man has searched out his similitude.
He is hidden to gods and men. He is a secret to all his creatures.
No man knoweth a name by which to call him.
His name is hidden. His name is a secret to all his children.
His names are without number.
His names are many; no man knoweth the number thereof.

In all kinds of Gaelic poetry from earliest times the triplet is a common device; in prayer the device gains an extra resonance from association with the Christian trinity.

A wavelet for thy form . . .

A wavelet for thy form,
A wavelet for thy voice,
A wavelet for thy sweet speech;

A wavelet for thy luck,
A wavelet for thy good,
A wavelet for thy health;

A wavelet for thy throat,
A wavelet for thy pluck,
A wavelet for thy graciousness;
Nine waves for thy graciousness.

From Spellcraft, *by Robin Skelton. A Canadian poet, Skelton had a lively belief and interest in practical magic. He described his book as a handbook of invocations, blessings, protections, spells, bindings and biddings. He argued that spellmaking is a skill and can be learned by anyone with sufficient psychic energy and powers of concentration.*

Journey Charm

I draw a protecting circle around myself with this rod and commend
   myself to God's grace,
against the sore stitch, against the sore bite,
against the fierce horror,
against the mighty dread that is hateful to everybody,
and against every evil that invades the land.
A victory charm I sing, a victory rod I carry,
victorious in word, victorious in deed, may this avail me.
May no nightmare disturb me, no powerful enemy oppress me,
may nothing dreadful ever befall my life.
But may the Almighty, the Son, and the Holy Ghost,
the Lord worthy of all honour,
as I have heard, the Creator of heaven, save me.
Abraham and Isaac and such men,
Moses and Jacob and David and Joseph,
and Eve and Anne and Elizabeth,
Zacharias and also Mary, the Mother of Christ,
And also the brothers Peter and Paul,
And also a thousand of the angels,
I call to my help against all foes.
They conduct and protect me and save my life,
They keep me and govern me,
Guiding my actions. A hope of glory,

a hand over my head be to me the host of the holy ones,
the band of victorious saints, the righteous angels.
I pray to all with glad mind
that for a blessing and protection,
Matthew be my helmet, Mark my coat of mail,
the strong light of my life, Luke my sword,
sharp and bright-edged, John my shield,
gloriously adorned, the Seraph of the roads.
I travel along, I meet friends,
all the glory of angels, the instruction of the blessed one.
I pray for good favour from the God of victory,
for a good voyage, a calm and light
wind to the shores. I have heard of winds
boiling waters. Ever secure
against all foes, I meet with friends,
that I may live in the peace of the almighty,
protected from the evil one who seeks my life,
established in the glory of the angels,
and in the holy land, the glory of the kingdom of heaven,
as long as I may live in this life. Amen.

Death Rite of the Gabon Pygmies
from Spellcraft

The animal runs, it passes, it dies. And it is the great cold.
It is the great cold of the night, it is the dark.
The bird flies, it passes, it dies. And it is the great cold.
It is the great cold of the night, it is the dark.
The fish flees, it passes, it dies. And it is the great cold.
It is the great cold of the night, it is the dark.
Man eats and sleeps. He dies. And it is the great cold.
It is the great cold of the night, it is the dark.
There is light in the sky, the eyes are extinguished, the star shines.
The cold is below, the light is on high.
The man has passed, the shade has vanished, the prisoner is free!
Khvum, Khvum, come in answer to our call!

A prayer to pagan gods for protection, for a long life and good fortune, and a charm against the hazards of life according to Henry, who attributes the original to the eighth-century abbot Fer fío macc Fabri.

I Invoke the Seven Daughters
trans. P. L. Henry

I invoke the seven daughters of the Sea
Who fashion the threads of the sons of long life.
May three deaths be removed from me,
Three lifetimes granted to me,
Seven waves of good fortune conferred on me!
May phantoms not harm me on my journey
In St Laserlian's corslet without hindrance!
May my name not be pledged in vain!
May old age come to me!
May death not come to me until I am old!

I invoke my silver champion
Who dies not, who will not die;
May a time be granted me
Of the excellence of white bronze!
May my form be arranged,
May my right be exalted,
May my strength be increased,
May my tomb not be readied,
May I not die on my journey,
May my return be confirmed!
May the headless serpent not seize me,
Nor the hard grey worm,
Nor the senseless chafer!

May no thief harm me,
Nor band of women,
Nor warrior band!
May increase of time come to me
From the King of the Universe!

I invoke seven-cycled Senach
Whom fairywomen suckled
On the paps of mystic lore.
May my seven candles not be quenched!
I am an invincible fortress,
I am an immovable rock,
I am a precious stone,
I am the symbol of seven treasures,
May my wealth be in hundreds,
My years in hundreds,
Each hundred after the other!

My benefits I call to me;
The grace of the Holy Spirit be upon me!
Domini est salus.
Christi est salus!
Super populum tuum, Domine, benedictio tua.

Joyous Death
from the Carmina Gadelica

Death with oil,
Death with joy,
Death with light,
Death with gladness,
Death with penitence.

Death without pain,
Death without fear,
Death without death,
Death without horror,
Death without grieving.

May the seven angels of the Holy Spirit
And the two guardian angels
Shield me this night and every night
Till light and dawn shall come;

Shield me this night and every night
Till light and dawn shall come.

The 'call and response' form still endures in the Gaelic song of Scotland, particularly in the waulking songs of the Hebrides. The form is originally, of course, a sea-shanty.

Sea Prayer
from the Carmina Gadelica

Helmsman
Blest be the boat.
Blest be the boat.
Blest be the boat.

Crew
God the Father bless her.
God the Son bless her.
God the Spirit bless her.

All
God the Father,
God the Son,
God the Spirit,
Bless the boat.

What can befall you
and God the Father with you?

No harm can befall us.

What can befall you
and God the Son with you?

No harm can befall us.

What can befall you
and God the Spirit with you?

No harm can befall us.

All
God the Father,
God the Son,
God the Spirit,
With us eternally.

What can cause you anxiety
And the God of the elements
over you?   No anxiety can be ours.

What can cause you anxiety
And the King of the elements
over you?   No anxiety can be ours.

What can cause you anxiety
And the Spirit of the elements
over you?   No anxiety can be ours.

> *All*
> The God of the elements,
> The King of the elements,
> The Spirit of the elements,
> Close over us,
> Ever eternally.

A Charm Rhyme

Anon.

This charme shall be said at night, or against night, about the place or feild, or about beasts without feild, and whosoever cometh in, he goeth not out for certaine.

On three crosses of a tree
three dead bodyes did hang,
two were theeves
the third was Christ
on whom our beleife is
Dismas and Gesmas
Christ amidst them was
Dismas to heaven went
Gesmas to hell was sent
Christ that died on the roode
for Marie's love that by him stood
and through the vertue of his blood
Jesus save us and our good
within and without
and all this place about
and through the vertue of his might
lett noe theefe enter in this night
no foote further in this place
than I upon goe
but at my bidding there be bound
to do all things that I bid them do
starke be their sinewes therewith
and their lives mightles
and their eyes sightless

dread and doubt
them enclose about
as a wall wrought of stone
so be the crampe in the ton
crampe and crookeing
and tault in their tooting
the might of the Trinity
save these goods and me
in the name of Jesus holy benedicité
all about our goods bee
within and without
and all place about!

O'Hehir is a contemporary American poet. Her Spells for Not Dying
Again *are poems which revivify ancient Egyptian traditions.*

Spell for Protecting the Heart after Death
Diana O'Hehir

My heart, my mother heart,
Heart of my living on earth.

Spirits, don't grab this heart with your fingers,
Don't steal and crush my heart.
It belongs to the living who walk about in the city.

When I was a child my heart shone in its egg,
My grown heart rose like a heron, cackled like a goose, my aged
    heart
Lay under the back-bent sky; was a dark stone in the sky's belt.

This heart belongs to the living who talk and make love in the city.

I kneel before a god who holds his tail in his hand.
Friends in the city, make a green scarab; place it over my heart,

Let my legs which are tied together be opened;
Let the chief of the gods spread his jaws for me, let the doors of
    Heaven be rolled ajar,
And my heart remain,
This heart that I have from my body.

The earliest known Irish example of a lorica, or breastplate; the term is applied to a genre of charm-prayers, derived from the idea of life as an armed struggle. A lorica, from the Latin, can be a cuirass or a metal shirt.

The Breastplate of Laidcenn

Help me, Unity in Trinity,
Trinity in Unity, take pity.

Help me, I beseech you, since I am
As if in peril on the great sea,
So that this year's plague does not
Drag me off, nor the world's vanity.

And this too I ask of the high powers
Of the host of heaven,
Not to leave me to be torn by the enemy
But to defend me now with powerful arms.

Let them go before me in the battle-line,
The armies of the heavenly host:
Cherubim and seraphim in their thousands,
Gabriel and Michael and their like.

I beseech the Thrones, Virtues, Archangels,
Principalities, Powers, and Angels
To defend me with their massed ranks
And to scatter my enemies.

Then I beseech the other champions,
The Patriarchs and the sixteen prophets,
The Apostles, pilots of the ship of Christ,
And all the martyrs, athletes of God,

That with their aid safety may surround me
And every evil pass from me.
May Christ make a firm covenant with me.
Let fear and fright fall on the foul fiends.

O God defend me everywhere
With your impregnable power and protection.
Deliver all my mortal limbs,
Guarding each with your protective shield,
So that the foul demons shall not hurl their darts
Into my side, as is their wont.

Deliver my skull, hair-covered head, and eyes,
Mouth, tongue, teeth, and nostrils,
Neck, breast, side, and limbs,
Joints, fat, and two hands.

Be a helmet of safety to my head,
To my crown covered with hair,
To my forehead, eyes, and triform brain,
To snout, lip, face, and temple,

To my chin, beard, eyebrows, ears,
Chaps, cheeks, septum, nostrils,
Pupils, irises, eyelids, and the like,
To gums, breath, jaws, gullet,

To my teeth, tongue, mouth, uvula, throat,
Larynx and epiglottis, cervix,
To the core of my head and gristle,
And to my neck may there be merciful protection.

Be then a most protective breastplate
For my limbs and innards,
So that you drive back from me the unseen
Nails of the shafts that foul fiends fashion.

Protect, O God, with your powerful breastplate
My shoulders with their shoulderblades and arms,
Protect my elbows, cups of the hand and hands,
fists, palms, fingers with their nails.

Protect my spine and ribs with their joints,
Back, ridge, and sinews with their bones;
Protect my skin and blood with kidneys,
The area of the buttocks, nates with thighs.

Protect my hams, calves, femurs,
Houghs and knees with knee-joints;
Protect my ankles with shins and heels,
Shanks, feet with their soles.

Protect my toes growing together,
With the tips of the toes and twice five nails;
Protect my breast, collarbone, and small breast,
Nipples, stomach, and navel.

Protect my belly, loins, and genitals,
Paunch, and the vital parts of my heart . . .

So that leaving the flesh I may escape the depths
And be able to fly to the heights,
And by the mercy of God be borne with joy
To be made anew in his kingdom on high.
Amen.

From A Celtic Miscellany, *edited and with translations by Kenneth Hurlstone Jackson. Herb charms are found in all traditions, in all cultures.*

A Charm with Yarrow

I will pick the smooth yarrow that my figure may be more elegant, that
my lips may be warmer, that my voice may be more cheerful; may my
voice be like a sunbeam, may my lips be like the juice of the strawberries.

May I be an island in the sea, may I be a hill on the land, may I be a star
when the moon wanes, may I be a staff to the weak one: I shall wound
every man, no man shall wound me.

The Nine Herbs Charm
trans. Gavin Chappell

Remember, Mugwort, what you revealed,
What you arranged at Regenmeld.
You are named Una, eldest of herbs,
Power against three and against thirty,
Power against poison and against venom,
Power against the enemy who travels over the earth.

And you, Plantain, mother of herbs,
Opening eastwards, inwardly mighty;
Over you carts creaked, over you women cantered,
Over you brides bridalled, over you bulls bellowed.
Then you weathered and withstood all;
So you withstand poison and venom
And the enemy who travels over the earth.

This herb is called Cress, it grew on a crag;
It stands against poison, stands against pain.
This is named nettle, it withstands venom,
Exiles the enemy, endures against poison.
This is the wort that fought with the worm,
This power against poison, power against infection,
Power against the enemy that travels over the earth.

Now, Betony, you banish the minor and major,
The major and minor, till he is remedied of both.

Remember, Camomile, what you made known,
What you ended at Alorford;
That he never let up his life for infection
After Camomile was cooked with his food.

This is the herb that is called Crab Apple;
The seal sent this over the spine of the ocean
As a nostrum for other noxious poisons.
These nine will work against nine poisons.

A serpent came sneaking, it struck a man;
Then Woden took nine wondrous staves,
Smote the snake so it split into nine pieces.
There ended the apple and poison
So never again would it enter a house.

Chervil and Fennel, fearsome pair,
The wise lord created these worts,
Holy in heaven, there was he hanged;
He set and sent them into seven worlds
To remedy all, the rich and the needy.

It stands against pain, struggles against poison,
Has might against three and against thirty,
Against devil's hand and against deception,
Against the witchcraft of the wicked ones.

These nine herbs have force against nine who fled glory,
Against nine venoms and against nine poisons,
Against the red venom, against the running venom,
Against the white venom, against the purple venom,

Against the yellow venom, against the green venom,
Against the black venom, against the blue venom,
Against the brown venom, against the bay venom,
Against worm-blister, against water-blister,
Against thorn-blister, against thistle-blister,
Against ice-blister, against poison-blister,
If any venom comes flying from the east,
Or any comes from the north,
Or any from the west comes upon the clans of men.

Christ stood over sicknesses of evil kinds.
Only I know the Running River
Where the nine snakes behold it near;
May all weeds now spring up as worts,
The seas dissolve, all salt water,
When I blow this bane from you.

Take mugwort, plantain that opens from the east, lamb's cress, betony, camomile, nettle, crab apple, chervil and fennel, and old soap. Grind the herbs into powder and mix them with the soap and the apple's juice. Make a paste of water and ashes, take the fennel, boil it in the paste and beat an egg into it before and after he (the patient) puts on the salve. Sing this spell over each herb, three times before he prepares it and also on the apple; and sing the same spell into the mouth and both ears and on the wound, before he puts on the salve.

From Norman Mailer's The Armies of the Night, *this is a text to be chanted by the Fugs, and by all participating in the great anti-war demonstration at the Pentagon in 1967. The intention was to levitate the building.*

October 21, 1967, Washington, D.C., U.S.A., Planet Earth

We freemen, of all colours of the spectrum, in the name of God, Ra, Jehovah, Anubis, Osiris, Tlaloc, Quetzalcoatl, Thoth, Ptah, Allah, Krishna, Chango, Chimeke, Chokwu, Olisa-Bulu-Uwa, Imales, Orisasu, Odudua, Kali, Shiva-Shakra, Great Spirit, Dionysus, Yahweh, Thor, Bacchus, Isia, Jesus Christ, Maitreya, Buddha, Rama do exorcize and cast out the EVIL which has walled and captured the pentacle of power and perverted its use to the need of the total machine and its child the hydrogen bomb and has suffered the people of the planet earth, the American people and creatures of the mountains, woods, streams, and oceans grievous mental and physical torture and the constant torment of the imminent threat of utter destruction.

We are demanding that the pentacle of power once again be used to serve the interests of GOD manifest in the world as man. We are embarking on a motion which is millennial in scope. Let this day, October 21, 1967, mark the beginning of suprapolitics.

By the act of reading this paper you are engaged in the Holy Ritual of Exorcism. To further participate focus your thought on the casting out of evil through the grace of GOD which is all (ours). A billion stars in a billion galaxies of space and time is the form of your power, and limitless is your name.

A Turning Verse for the Billions of Beings
Gary Snyder (from the Chinese)

We have spoken against the unknown words of the spell
that purifies the world
turning its virtue and power back   over
to those who died in wars – in the fields – on the seas
and to the billions of spirits in the realms of
form, of no-form, or in the realm of hot desire

Hail all true and grounded beings
in all directions,   in the realms of form,
of no-form, or of hot desire

hail all noble woke-up big-heart beings;
hail – great wisdom of the path that goes beyond

Mahāprajñāpāramitā

The Sibylline Oracles were widespread in the ancient world. Heraclitus tells us that the Sibyl was 'older than Orpheus' and that she reaches 'through thousands of years'. The oracle texts in this book are translated by J. J. Collins.

One God, the Creator
Sibylline Oracles

One God, who alone rules, exceedingly great unbegotten
but God alone, one highest of all, who made
heaven and sun and stars and moon
and fruitful earth and waves of water of sea
who alone is God, abiding as indomitable creator.
He established the shape of the form of mortals.
He himself mixed the nature of all, begetter of life.

The Battle of the Stars
Sibylline Oracles

I saw the threat of the burning sun among the stars
and the terrible wrath of the moon among the lightning flashes.
The stars travailed in battle; God bade them fight.
For over and against the sun long flames were in strife,
and the two-horned rush of the moon was changed.
Lucifer fought, mounted on the back of Leo.
Capricorn smote the ankle of the young Taurus,
and Taurus deprived Capricorn of his day of return.
Orion removed Libra so that it remained no more.
Virgo changed the destiny of Gemini in Aries.
The Pleiad no longer appeared and Draco rejected its belt.
Pisces submerged themselves in the girdle of Leo.
Cancer did not stand its ground, for it feared Orion.
Scorpio got under the tail because of terrible Leo,
and the dog star perished by the flame of the sun.
The strength of the mighty day star burned up Aquarius.
Heaven itself was roused until it shook up the fighters.
In anger it cast them headlong to earth.
Accordingly, stricken into the baths of ocean,
they quickly kindled the whole earth. But the sky remained starless.

Against the Pride of Kings
Sibylline Oracles

Men, why do you vainly think excessively proud thoughts
as if you were immortals, though your lordship is short,
and all wish to reign over mortals,
not perceiving that God himself hates
the love of lordship, and especially insatiable kings,
terrible and impious. He stirs up darkness against these,
because instead of good deeds and righteous thoughts
they all prefer purple mantles and cloaks,
desiring the wars, woes, and murders.
Imperishable God, who dwells in the sky, will utterly destroy these men
and make them short-lived, and will slay one here, another there.

A version of this prophecy was still being invoked in the nineteenth century by Karl Marx.

Eschatological Prophecy
Sibylline Oracles

No longer will there be deceitful gold or silver
or acquisition of land, or laborious slavery,
but one friendship and one manner for a merry people.
All will be in common, and one equal light of life.
On earth evil will sink into the wondrous sea.
Then the harvest of articulate men is near.
A strong necessity insists that these things be accomplished.
Then no other chance wayfarer will say
that the race of articulate men will cease to be, though they perish.
Then the holy nation will hold sway over the whole earth
for all ages, with their mighty children.

Fragmentary Oracle
Sibylline Oracles

O, O for the floating waters and all dry land
and the rising sun which will never set again.
All will obey him as he enters the world again
because it was the first to recognize his power also.

Riddles, when used in prayer, have the dual function of testing what the believer is supposed to know and prompting him or her to seek out deeper meanings.

A Riddle on the Name of God
Sibylline Oracles

I am the one who is, but you consider in your heart.
I am robed with heaven, draped around with sea,
the earth is the support of my feet, around my body is poured
the air, the entire chorus of stars revolves around me.
I have nine letters, I am of four syllables. Consider me.
The first three have two letters each.
The last has the rest, and five are consonants.
The entire number is twice eight
plus three hundred, three tens and seven. If you know who I am
you will not be uninitiated in my wisdom.

Hope and Trust

❦

Theognis of Megara got it about right when he said, 'Hope is the only good god remaining among mankind; the others have left and gone to Olympus.' He expresses here a widespread fear among believers that the gods, or God, have become so detached from our human concerns that they are now unreachable. It is not for nothing that 'Olympian' signifies a haughty, aloof detachment from the concerns of common people.

There are more prayers of hope spurred by grief or fear or a sense of being abandoned than there are prayers giving voice to simple confidence in God's goodness. Hope is a very human thing, the voice of a small unillusioned creature who yet thinks, in the face of persuasive evidence to the contrary, that he may be saved, or comforted, that wrongs will somehow be righted, that brute extinction is not what faces him or her. Prayers of hope, when they are not for deliverance from the large and petty injustices of this world, are typically prayers for salvation.

Camus says, in 'The Myth of Sisyphus', that we must learn to live beyond hopelessness and beyond hope. This is admirable advice, if austere: poor bare forked creatures that we are, most of us would find it difficult to follow. Hope, or rather hoping, is the natural condition of those who sense themselves powerless to effect change in their lives: the rich man, unless he is also a greedy man, does not buy lottery tickets. Hope is where you go when there is nothing you can do to rescue yourself from a predicament not of your making. Blind hope is a comfortless thing, and it is hardly surprising that the afflicted will seek a guarantor, a being with ears to listen and eyes to see, a compassionate heart with the power to make things well, or at least better.

Trust in the revealed word of God can issue in a brisk recapitulation of the covenant between God and man, a reminder that one expects certain rewards in return for keeping one's side of the bargain. There are prayers of a purer trust, too – prayers where the trust is not so much the point as that sense of assurance and exultation that issues from trust. In general, prayers of trust tend to give voice to a faith that is confidently understood, a nuanced and informed understanding where intellect, instinct and blind faith are comfortable in each other's company.

I am intrigued by the role of intermediaries in prayers of hope and trust. In the Gaelic traditions of Ireland and Scotland, where the most usual intermediary is Brigid, or Brigit, the prayer's focus is often an uncertain thing, tending more towards a familiar and fond sense of kinship with the saint than to the more formal business ostensibly in hand. It may or may not be of consequence here that Brigid as saint is a Christian overlaying of a well-regarded pre-Christian goddess whose cognates were widely venerated across pre-Christian Europe.

I leave the last words, as the first, to Theognis: 'But as long as man lives and sees the light of the sun, let him . . . count on Hope.'

CB

Theognis was a Greek poet and common-sense moralist of the sixth century BCE.

Hope is the only good god remaining . . .
Theognis of Megara

Hope is the only good god remaining among mankind; the others have left and gone to Olympus. Trust, a mighty god, has gone. Restraint has gone from men, and the Graces, my friend, have abandoned earth. Men's judicial oaths are no longer to be trusted, nor does anyone revere the immortal gods; the race of pious men has perished and men no longer recognize established rules of conduct or acts of piety. But as long as man lives and sees the light of the sun, let him show piety to the gods and count on Hope. Let him pray to the gods and burn splendid thigh bones, sacrificing to Hope first and last.

Levertov's father was a Hasidic Jew who converted to Christianity. She herself experienced a spiritual conversion to Christianity in 1984, and her poems from then to the end of her life wrestled with, among other things, problems of God and nothingness.

The Avowal
Denise Levertov

As swimmers dare
to lie face to the sky
and water bears them,
as hawks rest upon air
and air sustains them,
so would I learn to attain
freefall, and float
into Creator Spirit's deep embrace,
knowing no effort earns
that all-surrounding grace.

The hermit tradition, particularly in Ireland, was a rich source of prayer founded in an intense appreciation of the natural world.

All alone in my little cell . . .

All alone in my little cell, without the company of anyone;
  precious has been the pilgrimage before going to meet death.

A hidden secluded little hut, for the forgiveness of my sins; an
  upright, untroubled conscience toward holy heaven.

Sanctifying the body by good habits, trampling like a man upon
  it: with weak and tearful eyes for the forgiveness of my
  passions.

Passions weak and withered, renouncing this wretched world;
  pure and eager thoughts; let this be a prayer to God.

Heartfelt lament toward cloudy heaven, sincere and truly devout
  confessions, swift shower of tears.

A cold and anxious bed, like the lying down of a doomed man: a
  brief, apprehensive sleep as in danger, invocations frequent and
  early.

My food as befits my station, precious has been the captivity: my
  dinner, without doubt, would not make me full-blooded.

Dry bread weighed out, well we bow the head: water of the
  many coloured hillside, that is the drink I would take.

A bitter meagre dinner; diligently feeding the sick; keeping off strife and visits; a calm, serene conscience.

It would be desirable, a pure and holy blemish: cheeks withered and shrunken, a shriveled leathery skin.

Treading the paths of the Gospel; singing Psalms at every hour; an end of talking and long stories constant bending of the knees.

May my Creator visit me, my Lord, my King; may my spirit seek Him in the everlasting kingdom where he dwells.

Let this be the end of vice in the enclosures of churches; a lovely little cell among the graves, and I there alone.

All alone in my little cell, all alone thus; alone I came into the world, alone I shall go from it.

If by myself I have sinned through pride of this world, hear me lament for it all alone, O God!

The founder of Christian Science, Eddy believed God was a transcendent, infinite spirit beyond the limitations of materiality, and that illness, being an illusion, could be dealt with by means of a clearer perception of God.

O gentle presence . . .
Mary Baker Eddy

O gentle presence, peace and joy and power;
O Life divine, that owns each waiting hour,
Thou Love that guards the nestling's faltering flight!
Keep Thou my child on upward wing to-night.

Love is our refuge; only with mine eye
Can I behold the snare, the pit, the fall:
His habitation high is here, and nigh,
His arm encircles me, and mine, and all.

O make me glad for every scalding tear,
For hope deferred, ingratitude, disdain!
Wait, and love more for every hate, and fear
No ill, – since God is good, and loss is gain.

Beneath the shadow of His mighty wing;
In that sweet secret of the narrow way,
Seeking and finding, with the angels sing:
'Lo, I am with you alway,' – watch and pray.

No snare, no fowler, pestilence or pain;
No night drops down upon the troubled breast,
When heaven's aftersmile earth's tear-drops gain,
And mother finds her home and heavenly rest.

From the Leabhar Breac, *an early Irish manuscript. The lark is often associated with supernatural powers in the Irish and in other traditions; here it is the link between earth and heaven.*

The Lark Sings
trans. Ciarán Mac Murchaidh

The knowing lark sings –
I go out to look at her
to see the gaping beak
high up in the bright clouds of heaven.

I will direct my psalms
towards the bright clouds of heaven,
for my unceasing protection,
and for the cleansing of my sins.

Smart was for many years confined to an asylum, suffering from 'religious mania'. Samuel Johnson said of him, 'I'd as lief pray with Kit Smart as anyone else.' This edited extract from his most-quoted piece shows a profound, even startling, religious sensibility at work.

from Jubilate Agno, Fragment B
Christopher Smart

For I will consider my cat Jeoffry.

For he is the servant of the living God, duly and daily serving Him.

For at the first glance of the glory of God in the East he worships in his way.

For this is done by wreathing his body seven times round with elegant quickness.

For then he leaps up to catch the musk, which is the blessing of God upon his prayer . . .

For having consider'd God and himself he will consider his neighbour.

For if he meets another cat he will kiss her in kindness . . .

For when his day's work is done his business more properly begins.

For he keeps the Lord's watch in the night against the adversary.

For he counteracts the powers of darkness by his electrical skin and glaring eyes.

For he counteracts the Devil, who is death, by brisking about the life . . .

For he knows that God is his saviour.

For there is nothing sweeter than his peace when at rest.

For there is nothing brisker than his life when in motion.

For he is of the Lord's poor and so indeed is he called by benevolence perpetually – Poor Jeoffry! poor Jeoffry! the rat has bit thy throat.

For I bless the name of the Lord Jesus that Jeoffry is better.

For the divine spirit comes about his body to sustain it in complete cat . . .

For by stroking of him I have found out electricity.

For I perceived God's light about him both wax and fire.

For the Electrical fire is the spiritual substance, which God sends from heaven to sustain the bodies of both man and beast.

For God has blessed him in the variety of his movements . . .

For he can tread to all the measures upon the music.

For he can swim for life.

For he can creep.

Words given to Socrates at the end of the Phaedrus. *Pan, generally considered god of the woods and the wild, seems an odd choice of recipient for this address.*

O beloved Pan . . .
Plato

O beloved Pan, and all the other gods of this place, grant that I may become beautiful in my inner soul, and that all my possessions in the world may be harmonious with my inner self. May I consider the wise man rich, and may I have such wealth as only a man of self-discipline can master or endure.

Padmasambhava is said to have introduced Tantric Buddhism to Tibet.
When he passed, he departed to the west in a body of pure light to the
buddha-field known as the Glorious Copper-coloured Mountain.

The Chariot of Joy and Good Fortune
Jigdral Yeshe Dorje

Self-manifested pure appearance, vajra space of supreme bliss,
spontaneously-arisen Akanishta, the dance of interwoven magical displays,
the most excellent ocean of infinite buddha-realms.

May I be born at The Glorious Copper-Coloured Mountain,
at the summit of the delightful imperial mountain of rubies,
a tiered palace of jewelled domes, superb and wondrous in its beautiful
    design.

May I be born at The Glorious Copper-Coloured Mountain,
amid pastures and sandalwood forests,
fresh grassy regions of turquoise gems and many-coloured lotus blos-
    soms,
with smiling pollen hearts boasting in youthful laughter.

May I be born at The Glorious Copper-Coloured Mountain,
with rivers of amrita threaded with camphor-scented water
cascading delightfully and swirling into pools
where youthful dancers frolic, moving this way and that.

May I be born at The Glorious Copper-Coloured Mountain –
from the lattice openings of the rainbow pavilion
a sprinkling rain of flowers falls, garlands of atoms
in which great heroes sport in their dance of bliss.

May I be born at The Glorious Copper-Coloured Mountain.
With most excellent abundances of numerous sense qualities,
clouds of dakinis, all beautiful, all lavishly adorned,
spread endlessly into the upper reaches of the sky.

May I be born at The Glorious Copper-Coloured Mountain.
At the heart of the ranked assembly of knowledge-holders
the supreme victor, Pema Jyungnay,
proclaims in the voice of a magnificent lion the profound secret,

(May I be born at The Glorious Copper-Coloured Mountain)
saying 'I am the essence of all buddhas';
with the incomparable power of knowledge, love and wisdom,
he undertakes to tame accordingly the various kinds of endless beings.

May I be born at The Glorious Copper-Coloured Mountain.
When this limitless treasury, an ocean of noble qualities,
is merely a memory, then one is established in that realm
which bears the splendour and blessings of the wheel of wondrous activity.

May I be born at The Glorious Copper-Coloured Mountain.
At this very moment, travelling instantaneously
to the beautiful city of Lotus Light, the pure realm of space,
in accordance with the example of your liberation, the
    accomplishment of the two benefits according to one's wishes,
May I become as you, incomparable Guru.

May all beings benefit

Étienne de Vignolles, called La Hire, the 'Growler', fought alongside Jeanne d'Arc, was of a bad-tempered disposition and is commemorated as the face on the jack of hearts in the French deck of cards.

La Hire's Prayer

I pray that my God will do for La Hire what La Hire would do for Him, if God were Captain and La Hire was God.

Surah 11.41: Prayer of Noah
Qur'an

In God's name be the course and the mooring: let us embark.

Appointed Archbishop of Canterbury, but prohibited at first, by King John, from returning to his native England, Langton would eventually prevail on the king to sign the Magna Carta.

Veni, Sancte Spiritus
Stephen Langton, trans. John Austin

Come, Holy Ghost,

send down those beams,
which sweetly flow in silent streams
from Thy bright throne above.

O come, Thou Father of the poor;
O come, Thou source of all our store,
come, fill our hearts with love.

O Thou, of comforters the best,
O Thou, the soul's delightful guest,
the pilgrim's sweet relief.

Rest art Thou in our toil, most sweet
refreshment in the noonday heat;
and solace in our grief.

O blessed Light of Life Thou art;
fill with thy light the inmost heart
of those who hope in thee.

Without Thy Godhead nothing can
have any price or worth in man,
nothing can harmless be.

Lord, wash our sinful stains away,
refresh from heaven our barren clay,
our wounds and bruises heal.

To Thy sweet yoke our stiff necks bow,
warm with Thy fire our hearts of snow,
our wandering feet recall.

Grant to Thy faithful, dearest Lord,
whose only hope is Thy sure word,
the sevenfold gifts of grace.

Grant us in life Thy grace that we
in peace may die, and ever be
in joy before Thy face.

Amen. Alleluia.

Brontë might fairly be described as a Gothic angelicist; one might, at a stretch, consider this a Christian prayer.

The Visionary
Emily Brontë

Silent is the house: all are laid asleep:
One alone looks out o'er the snow-wreaths deep,
Watching every cloud, dreading every breeze
That whirls the wildering drift, and bends the groaning trees.

Cheerful is the hearth, soft the matted floor;
Not one shivering gust creeps through pane or door;
The little lamp burns straight, its rays shoot strong and far:
I trim it well, to be the wanderer's guiding-star.

Frown, my haughty sire! chide, my angry dame!
Set your slaves to spy; threaten me with shame:
But neither sire nor dame, nor prying serf shall know,
What angel nightly tracks that waste of frozen snow.

What I love shall come like visitant of air,
Safe in secret power from lurking human snare;
What loves me, no word of mine shall e'er betray,
Though for faith unstained my life must forfeit pay.

Burn, then, little lamp; glimmer straight and clear –
Hush! a rustling wing stirs, methinks, the air:
He for whom I wait, thus ever comes to me;
Strange Power! I trust thy might; trust thou my constancy.

The scallop shell was the emblem of those who had undertaken the pilgrimage to Santiago de Compostela in Spain. Ralegh's acquaintance with Spain seems to have been confined to killing such of its sailors and soldiers, Christians all, as he encountered.

The Pilgrimage
Sir Walter Ralegh

Give me my scallop-shell of quiet,
My staff of faith to walk upon,
My scrip of joy, immortal diet,
My bottle of salvation,
My gown of glory, hope's true gage;
And thus I'll take my pilgrimage . . .

Even Such Is Time
Sir Walter Ralegh

Even such is time, that takes in trust
Our youth, our joys, our all we have,
And pays us but with earth and dust;
Who, in the dark and silent grave,
When we have wandered all our ways,
Shuts up the story of our days.
But from this earth, this grave, this dust,
My God shall raise me up, I trust.

According to Newbolt in his prefatory note, 'This myth, of Egyptian origin, formed part of the instruction given to those initiated in the Orphic mysteries, and written versions of it were buried with the dead.'

The Final Mystery
Sir Henry Newbolt

Hear now, O Soul, the last command of all –
When thou hast left thine every mortal mark,
And by the road that lies beyond recall
Won through the desert of the Burning Dark,
Thou shalt behold within a garden bright
A well, beside a cypress ivory-white.

Still is that well, and in its waters cool
White, white and windless, sleeps that cypress tree:
Who drinks but once from out her shadowy pool
Shall thirst no more to all eternity.
Forgetting all, by all forgotten clean,
His soul shall be with that which hath not been.

But thou, though thou be trembling with thy dread,
And parched with thy desire more fierce than flame,
Think on the stream wherefrom thy life was fed,
And that diviner fountain whence it came.
Turn thee and cry – behold, it is not far –
Unto the hills where living waters are.

'Lord, though I lived on earth, the child of earth,
Yet was I fathered by the starry sky:
Thou knowest I came not of the shadows' birth,

Let me not die the death that shadows die.
Give me to drink of the sweet spring that leaps
From Memory's fount, wherein no cypress sleeps.'

Then shalt thou drink, O Soul, and therewith slake
The immortal longing of thy mortal thirst;
So of thy Father's life shalt thou partake,
And be for ever that thou wert at first.
Lost in remembered loves, yet thou more thou
With them shalt reign in never-ending *Now*.

A one-time Anglican cleric, a poet, political and homosexual activist and mystic, Carpenter strove to unite his socialism with the insights he gained from a study of the Bhagavad Gita. He was profoundly influenced by Whitman's ecstatic visions of democracy as a spiritual force. He died in 1929.

By the Shore
Edward Carpenter

All night by the shore.
The obscure water, the long white lines of advancing foam, the
    rustle and thud, the panting sea-breaths, the pungent sea-smell,
The great slow air moving from the distant horizon, the immense
    mystery of space and the soft canopy of the clouds!

The swooning thuds go on – the drowse of ocean goes on:
The long inbreaths – the short sharp outbreaths – the silence
    between.

I am a bit of the shore: the waves feed upon me, they come
    pasturing over me;
I am glad, O waves, that you come pasturing over me.

I am a little arm of the sea: the same tumbling swooning dream
    goes on – I feel the waves all around me, I spread myself
    through them.
How delicious! I spread and spread. The waves tumble through
    and over me – they dash through my face and hair.
The night is dark overhead: I do not see them, but I touch them
    and hear their gurgling laughter.

The play goes on!
The strange expanding indraughts go on!
Suddenly I am the Ocean itself: the great soft wind creeps over
    my face.
I am in love with the wind – I reach my lips to its kisses.
How delicious! all night and ages and ages long to spread myself
    to the gliding wind!
But now (and ever) it maddens me with its touch, I arise and
    whirl in my bed, and sweep my arms madly along the shores.

I am not sure any more which my own particular bit of shore is;
All the bays and inlets know me; I glide along in and out under
    the sun by the beautiful coast-line;
My hair floats leagues behind me; millions together my children
    dash against my face;
I hear what they say and am marvellously content.

All night by the shore;
And the sea is a sea of faces.
The long white lines come up – face after face comes and falls
    past me –
Thud after thud. Is it pain or joy?
Face after face – endless!

I do not know; my sense numbs; a trance is on me –
I am becoming detached!
I am a bit of the shore:
The waves feed upon me, they pasture all over me, my feeling is
    strangely concentrated at every point where they touch me;
I am glad, O waves, that you come pasturing over me.

I am detached, I disentangle myself from the shore;
I have become free – I float out and mingle with the rest.
The pain, the acute clinging desire, is over – I feel beings like
    myself all around me, I spread myself through and through
    them, I am merged in a sea of contact.
Freedom and equality are a fact. Life and joy seem to have begun
    for me.

The play goes on!
Suddenly I am the great living Ocean itself – the awful Spirit of
    Immensity creeps over my face.

I am in love with it. All night and ages and ages long and for ever I
    pour my soul out to it in love.
I spread myself out broader and broader for ever, that I may
    touch it and be with it everywhere.
There is no end. But ever and anon it maddens me with its touch.
    I arise and sweep away my bounds.

I know but I do not care any longer which my own particular
    body is – all conditions and fortunes are mine.
By the ever-beautiful coast-line of human life, by all shores, in all
    climates and countries, by every secluded nook and inlet,
Under the eye of my beloved Spirit I glide:
O joy! for ever, ever, joy!
I am not hurried – the whole of eternity is mine;

With each one I delay, with each one I dwell – with you I dwell.
The warm breath of each life ascends past me;
I take the thread from the fingers that are weary, and go on with
    the work;

The secretest thoughts of all are mine, and mine are the secretest
    thoughts of all.

All night by the shore;
And the fresh air comes blowing with the dawn.
The mystic joy fades – but my joy fades not.
I arise and cast a stone into the water (O sea of faces I cast this
    poem among you) – and turn landward over the rustling
    beach.

A parish priest at Credenhill near Hereford, England, for ten years,
Traherne spent the remainder of his life as private chaplain to Sir Orlando
Bridgeman, Lord Keeper of the Seals to Charles II. Traherne's Centuries
of Meditations, *of which the following is an extract from one entry, was*
first published in 1908, 234 years after his death.

from The Third Century
Thomas Traherne

The corn was orient and immortal wheat, which never should be
reaped, nor was ever sown. I thought it had stood from everlasting
to everlasting. The dust and stones of the street were as precious as
gold. The gates were at first the end of the world, the green trees
when I saw them first through one of the gates transported and
ravished me; their sweetness and unusual beauty made my heart
to leap, and almost mad with ecstasy, they were such strange and
wonderful things. The men! O what venerable and reverend creatures
did the aged seem! Immortal cherubims! And the young men glittering and sparkling angels and maids strange seraphic pieces of life
and beauty! Boys and girls tumbling in the streets, and playing, were
moving jewels. I knew not that they were born or should die. But all
things abided eternally as they were in their proper places. Eternity
was manifest in the light of the day, and something infinite behind
everything appeared: which talked with my expectation and moved
my desire. The city seemed to stand in Eden, or to be built in Heaven.
The streets were mine, the temple was mine, the people were mine,
their clothes and gold and silver was mine, as much their sparkling
eyes, fair skins, and ruddy faces. The skies were mine, and so were
the sun and moon and stars, and all the world was mine, and I the
only spectator and enjoyer of it. I knew no churlish proprieties, nor
bounds nor divisions; but all proprieties and divisions were mine: all

treasures and the possessors of them. So that with much ado I was corrupted; and made to learn the dirty devices of this world. Which I now unlearn, and become as it were a little child again, that I may enter into the Kingdom of God.

Wisdom of This World

To think long on God is to be drawn from what seems a lesser into what seems a greater world, the satisfaction of an all-too-human yearning for some final certainty, some resting place for restless thought. It is a very short step in some ways, this move from what is merely contingent towards what seems reassuringly eternal and fixed; what is constantly surprising to me is the extent to which, for many believers, this step becomes in fact irrevocable, a negation of that very world in which their being is grounded. There are of course those who negotiate backwards and forwards between the contingent and the eternal domains, but there are all too many for whom the idea of God slides into an indifference towards, a neglect of, even a hatred of this actual world in which we live.

The great thing about this world is the very *hereness* of it, its material heft and savour, its vast reassurance to the incarnate being who, with one kind or another of unease, is plagued by the restlessness of mind. There may well be other spheres of being, there may well be other and *greater* spheres of being, we can allow for that possibility if for no better reason than that we can entertain the thought of it, and many of us have intuitions of it; but this is the world we are framed for, and like countless others I am no more disposed to turn my attention from it than I am capable, by an act of will, of ceasing to draw breath.

Many prayers pay some lip service to God's creation, but their loving attention to this world of ours is often no more than notional. By contrast, there are some prayers that resonate with gratitude for the small daily miracle of life, the larger miracle of this world we share. In this section I have gathered prayers that share a lively sense of joy or sorrow in, or gratitude for, this world that is miracle and home enough. When these prayers are addressed to a god, they ask no more of God than to be permitted to acknowledge the grace of being in this life, this sudden gift. Even in sorrow or pain they acknowledge the dignity of being human, on this earth and of it.

A baffling, sophisticated prayer from Africa, described by its translator as a 'Pygmy hymn'. Perhaps a gloss on the opening of Genesis; perhaps something else entirely.

In the Beginning
trans. A. C. Young

In the beginning was God,
Today is God,
Tomorrow will be God,
Who can make an image of God?
He has no body.
He is the word which comes out of your mouth.
That word! It is no more,
It is the past, and still it lives!
So is God.

This is one of a great many Native American prayers with profound affinities to the Buddhist world view.

Great Spirit

Great Spirit, the star nations all over the heavens are Yours,
And Yours are the grasses of the earth.
You are older than all need,
Older than all pain and prayer.

Great Spirit, teach us to walk the soft earth as relatives to all that live.

Atheist Prayer
Richard Packham

Our powers are within,
Whatever be their name.
What they have done, what still may come,
This earth can yet be as Heaven.
Live then this day, and without dread,
And forgive your own trespasses
As you forgive those who trespass against you.
And be not led into temptation,
But flee away from evil,
For Time is the Healer,
With power to restore me,
Forever and ever, Amen.

Artemis, twin sister to Apollo, was the virginal goddess of the moon and the hunt. Penelope's plea for death, prompted by despair at having lost her husband, is addressed to the goddess, presumably, as a reliable marks-woman; Artemis might be considered an odd choice for such a wifely prayer.

from Odyssey 18.202
Homer, trans. Ian Johnston

[Penelope] when she had her fill of weeping, the queen made especial prayer to Artemis:

Artemis, Potna Thea (goddess queen), Daughter of Zeus, how glad should I be if here and now you would plant an arrow in my breast and take my life away all at once – or else if a whirlwind might snatch me up, carry me on through dusky pathways and cast me down at the issuing-place of backward-flowing Okeanos . . . In self-same fashion may the Olympians cause me to vanish from the world, or else let Artemis slay me with her arrows, so that I may pass beneath cheerless earth with Odysseus himself in my heart's vision. May I never gladden the heart of a man less noble.

Herbert, the great metaphysical poet, whose mother was patron to John Donne, spent the latter part of his life as rector in Bemerton, near Salisbury.

The Collar
George Herbert

I struck the board, and cry'd, 'No more;
    I will abroad.'
What, shall I ever sigh and pine?
My lines and life are free; free as the rode,
Loose as the winde, as large as store.
    Shall I be still in suit?
Have I no harvest but a thorn
To let me bloud, and not restore
What I have lost with cordiall fruit?
    Sure there was wine
Before my sighs did drie it; there was corn
Before my tears did drown it.
Is the yeare onely lost to me?
Have I no bayes to crown it,
No flowers, no garlands gay? all blasted,
    All wasted?
Not so, my heart; but there is fruit,
    And thou hast hands.
Recover all thy sigh-blown age
On double pleasures; leave thy cold dispute
Of what is fit and not; forsake thy cage,
    Thy rope of sands,
Which pettie thoughts have made; and made to thee
Good cable, to enforce and draw,

And be thy law,
While thou didst wink and wouldst not see.
Away! take heed;
I will abroad.
Call in thy death's-head there, tie up thy fears;
He that forbears
To suit and serve his need
Deserves his load.
But as I rav'd and grew more fierce and wilde
At every word,
Me thought I heard one calling, 'Childe';
And I reply'd, 'My Lord.'

A disciple of Wordsworth, sometime Dean of Westminster, later appointed Protestant archbishop of his native Dublin, Chenevix Trench reluctantly oversaw the disestablishment of the Church of Ireland in 1869.

If there had anywhere appeared in space . . .
Richard Chenevix Trench

If there had anywhere appeared in space
Another place of refuge, where to flee,
Our hearts had taken refuge in that place,
and not with Thee.

For we against creation's bars had beat
Like prisoned eagles, through great worlds had sought
Though but a foot of ground to plant our feet,
Where Thou wert not.

And only when we found in earth and air,
In heaven or hell, that such might nowhere be –
That we could not flee from Thee anywhere,
We fled to Thee.

*The remarkable twelfth-century polymath Hildegard was a visionary
and theologian, a composer of plainchant and antiphons, an adviser to
kings and popes; she wrote treatises about natural history and is the first
composer whose biography is known.*

Responsory for Confessors
Hildegard of Bingen, trans. Barbara Newman

Superlative actors! How noble
the play, how splendid
your costume, how lofty
your role! See how a man
plays Christ. He steps forth
to bind and to loose
the wayward
with the wayfaring.
To white and to black
he gives beauty,
he lifts burdens away.

Not only with angels
do you sing your part,
but you know the sites
of the firmest foundations
before you have built them.
Great is your honour!
To white and to black
you give beauty,
you lift burdens away.

A Sufi shaykh of the thirteenth and fourteenth centuries, Maneri is still venerated in both the Hindu and Muslim traditions in India as an enlightened master. His principal published legacy is The Hundred Letters.

Be careful, O man . . .
Sharafuddin Maneri, trans. Paul Jackson SJ

Be careful, O man with head bowed in foolishness,
For the sake of the world you abandoned your faith.
How long will you worry about what you eat or wear?
How long will you be concerned about name and fame?
Why are you proud of commanding the respect of a demon?
You have gone mad! You yourself have become a demon!
When from this furnace you reach that rose garden
It will seem that you had never seen this furnace.

O heart . . .
Sharafuddin Maneri, trans. Paul Jackson SJ

O heart, if you go seeking along His way,
Look carefully in front and behind, and only then proceed!
Look at the travellers who have arrived at His threshold,
Generation after generation have arrived together!
How do you know about which road to take?
How can you know which one leads to His threshold?
For every single particle there is a particular entrance:
Yes, for each particle there is indeed a separate road to Him!

Dharma, sometimes translated (from the Sanskrit) as 'truth' or 'the way', is the underlying order in nature, and also has the sense of life lived in harmony with that order. Getsudo was a Zen monk of the fourteenth century.

I Moved across the Dharma-Nature
Getsudo

I moved across the Dharma-nature
The earth was buoyant, marvellous,
That very night, whipping its iron horse,
The void galloped into Cloud Street.

Muso Kokushi was known in Japan as the National Zen Master. He founded the Reikisan Tenriyu-ji temple of the Rinzai sect in 1339.

Many Times the Mountains Have Turned
Muso Kokushi

Many times the mountains have turned from green to yellow –
So much for the capricious earth!
Dust in your eyes, the triple world is narrow;
Nothing on your mind, your chair is wide enough.

Cheville *(for Kaikhosru Sorabji)*
Hugh MacDiarmid

Who remembers the Great flood? The scope
Of the waters and their deafening din
Towering like God over the spirits of men,
Flocks, forests, and villages cast to the deep,
Who can sustain the menace of Nature
And praise forces to which life is straw
– Or glimpse them without seeming to outgrow
His mortality in huge recognition?
Tiger-cub torrent, shall I watch you and try
To think of all water is to the world? –
Seeing, and sorry for, all drowned things, sorry
Yet with, *cheville*, a sense of God's glory.

Born in 1207 in what is now Afghanistan, Rumi was a Sufi master whose great theme was the soul's longing for that God from whom it has become separated. His teachings, particularly in the Mathnawi, *have still a great resonance among people of all religions and none.*

There Is Some Kiss We Want
Jelaluddin Rumi, trans. Coleman Barks

There is some kiss we want
with our whole lives,
the touch of Spirit on the body.

Seawater begs the pearl
to break its shell.

And the lily, how passionately
it needs some wild Darling!

At night, I open the window
and ask the moon to come
and press its face into mine.
Breathe into me.

Close the language-door,
and open the love-window.

The moon won't use the door,
only the window.

The language of the Aztec empire was Nahuatl. In A Scattering of Jades, *from which the next two prayers come, Thelma D. Sullivan collects a wide range of Aztec prayers, poems and stories.*

Be Indomitable, O My Heart!
Nahuatl, trans. Rita Wilensky

Be indomitable, O my heart!
Love only the sunflower;
It is the flower of the Giver-of-Life!
What can my heart do?
Have we come, have we sojourned here on earth in vain?

As the flowers wither, I shall go.
Will there be nothing of my glory ever?
Will there be nothing of my fame on earth?
At most songs, at most flowers.
What can my heart do?
Have we come, have we sojourned on earth in vain?

Our Lord

Nahuatl, trans. Rita Wilensky

Our Lord,
Ever-present, ever-close,
Thinks as he pleases,
Does as he pleases,
He mocks us.
As he wishes, so he wills.
He has us in the middle of his hand
And rolls us about,
Like pebbles we spin and bounce,
He flings us every which way.
We offer him diversion,
He laughs at us.

The Great Sea Has Set Me in Motion
Inuit prayer song

The great sea has set me in motion,
Set me adrift,
And I move as a weed in the river.

The arch of sky
And mightiness of storms
Encompasses me,
And I am left
Trembling with joy.

Almost nothing is known about Porete except that she was the author of a book called The Mirror of Simple Souls, *also known as* The Mirror of Simple Annihilated Souls. *She was burnt at the stake for heresy in 1310, after refusing to remove her book from circulation.*

Here Speaks Love
Marguerite Porete

Among you actives and contemplatives and you who are perhaps annihilated by true love, who will hear some of the powers of the pure love, the noble love, the high love of the Free Soul, and how the Holy Spirit put His sail in the Soul, as if in His ship, I beg you out of love, says Love, to listen carefully with the subtle understanding within you and with great diligence, for otherwise all those if they be not so who will hear this will understand badly

Pearse, executed for his part in the Easter Rising of 1916, had mystical Christian inclinations reminiscent of those of John of the Cross.

The Wayfarer
Patrick Pearse

The beauty of the world hath made me sad,
This beauty that will pass;
Sometimes my heart hath shaken with great joy
To see a leaping squirrel in a tree,
Or a red lady-bird upon a stalk,
Or little rabbits in a field at evening,
Lit by a slanting sun.
Or some green hill where shadows drifted by
Some quiet hill where mountainy man hath sown
And soon would reap; near to the gate of Heaven;
Or children with bare feet upon the sands
Of some ebbed sea, or playing on the streets
Of little towns in Connacht,
Things young and happy.
And then my heart hath told me:
These will pass,
Will pass and change, will die and be no more,
Things bright and green, things young and happy;
And I have gone upon my way
Sorrowful.

A text which embodies the central tenets of mainstream Buddhism, usually attributed to the Buddha.

Buddhist Prayer for Peace

May all beings everywhere plagued
with sufferings of body and mind
quickly be freed from their illnesses.
May those who are frightened cease to be afraid,
and those who are bound be made free.
May the powerless find power,
and may people think of befriending one another.
May those who find themselves in trackless, fearful wilderness –
the children, the aged, the unprotected –
be guarded by beneficent celestials,
and may they swiftly attain Buddhahood.

Cawein, born in Kentucky, published a poem called 'Waste Land' in 1913, nine years before T. S. Eliot's poem of the same name appeared. Scholars have suggested other connections between the works of the two men.

Sibylline
Madison Julius Cawein

There is a glory in the apple boughs
Of silver moonlight; like a torch of myrrh,
Burning upon an altar of sweet vows,
Dropped from the hand of some wan worshipper:
And there is life among the apple blooms
Of whisp'ring winds; as if a god addressed
The flamen from the sanctuary glooms
With secrets of the bourne that hope had guessed,
Saying: 'Behold, a darkness which illumes,
A waking which is rest.'

There is a blackness in the apple trees
Of tempest; like the ashes of an urn
Hurt hands have gathered upon blistered knees,
With salt of tears, out of the flames that burn:
And there is death among the blooms, that fill
The night with breathless scent, – as when, above
The priest, the vision of his faith doth will
Forth from his soul the beautiful form thereof, –
Saying: 'Behold! A silence never still;
The other form of love.'

from Surah 24
Qur'an

God is the light of the heavens and the earth. The likeness of His light
is as a niche where a lamp burns – the lamp in a glass and the glass, as
it were, a star for brilliance. The lamp is kindled from a blessed tree,
an olive neither of the east nor of the west, the oil of which is almost
incandescent of itself without the touch of fire. Light upon light. God
guides to His light whom He wills.

A responsory is an anthem said or sung after a lesson by a soloist and choir alternately.

Responsory for Patriarchs and Prophets
Hildegard of Bingen, trans. Barbara Newman

O flourishing
roots of the tree of wonders
(no longer the tree of crimes),
a cascade of dappled shadow
rained on your planting.

And you, fire-breathing
voice, chewing
the cud of the world, racing
to the touchstone that
topples hell:
rejoice in your captain!

Rejoice in him whom many,
though they called on him ardently,
saw not upon this earth.
Rejoice in your captain!

Prayer
Carol Ann Duffy

Some days, although we cannot pray, a prayer
utters itself. So, a woman will lift
her head from the sieve of her hands and stare
at the minims sung by a tree, a sudden gift.

Some nights, although we are faithless, the truth
enters our hearts, that small familiar pain;
then a man will stand stock-still, hearing his youth
in the distant Latin chanting of a train.

Pray for us now. Grade I piano scales
console the lodger looking out across
a Midlands town. The dusk, and someone calls
a child's name as though they named their loss.

Darkness outside. Inside the radio's prayer –
Rockall. Malin. Dogger. Finisterre.

Vaughan attributed his spiritual awakening at the age of thirty-four to the poet and divine George Herbert, who had died twenty years previously.

Quickness
Henry Vaughan

False life! A foil and no more, when
Wilt thou be gone?
Thou foul deception of all men
That would not have the true come on.

Thou art a Moon-like toil; a blinde
Self-posing state;
A dark contest of waves and winde;
A meer tempestuous debate.

Life is a fix'd, discerning light,
A knowing joy;
No chance, or fit; but ever bright,
And calm and full, yet doth not cloy.

'Tis such a blissful thing, that still
doth vivifie,
and shine and smile, and hath the skill
to please without eternity.

Thou art a toylsom Mole, or less
A moving mist
But life is, what none can express,
A quickness, which my God hath kist.

Maimonides, who lived in Spain and Egypt in the latter half of the twelfth century, was a rabbi, physician and philosopher, one of a number of such Jewish figures who had an influence in the Christian and Muslim spheres in the Middle Ages.

Daily Prayer of a Physician
attrib. Moses Maimonides, trans. Harry Friedenwald

. . . Grant that my patients have confidence in me and my art and follow my directions and counsel. Remove from their midst all charlatans and the whole host of officious relatives and know-all nurses, cruel people who arrogantly frustrate the wisest purposes of our art and often lead Thy creatures to their death.

Should those who are wiser than I wish to improve and instruct me, let my soul gratefully follow their guidance; for vast is the extent of our art. Should conceited fools, however, censure me, then let love for my profession steel me against them, so that I remain steadfast without regard for age, for reputation, or for honour, because surrender would bring to Thy creatures sickness and death.

Imbue my soul with gentleness and calmness when older colleagues, proud of their age, wish to displace me or to scorn me or disdainfully to teach me. May even this be of advantage to me, for they know many things of which I am ignorant, but let not their arrogance give me pain. For they are old and old age is not master of the passions. I also hope to attain old age upon this earth, before Thee, Almighty God!

Let me be contented in everything except in the great science of my profession. Never allow the thought to arise in me that I have attained to sufficient knowledge, but vouchsafe to me the strength, the leisure and the ambition ever to extend my knowledge. For art is great, but the mind of man is ever-expanding . . .

More, author of Utopia, *was beheaded by Henry VIII for refusing to accept the monarch as head of the Church of England. He was canonized St Thomas More in 1935, and made patron of lawyers and statesmen.*

A Prayer
Sir Thomas More

Grant, I thee pray, such heat into mine heart
That to this love of thine shall be equal;
Grant me from Satan's service to astart,
With whom me rueth so long to have been thrall;
Grant me, good Lord and Creator of all,
The flame to quench of all sinful desire
And in thy love set all mine heart afire.

That when the journey of this deadly life
My silly ghost had finished, and thence
Departen must without his fleshly wife,
Alone into his Lorde's high presence,
He may thee find, O well of indulgence,
In thy lordship not as a lord, but rather
As a very tender, loving father.

The Hunters
Native American

There were but two beneath the sky –
The thing I came to kill, and I.
I, under cover, quietly
Watched him sense Eternity.
From quivering brush to pointed nose
My gun to shoulder level rose
And then I felt (I could not see)
Far off a hunter watching me.
I slowly put my rifle by,
For there were two who had to die –
The thing I wished to kill, and I.

The author of this sixteenth-century song is unknown, but the English composers Taverner, Tye and Sheppard all based masses on the tune.

Westron Wynde
Anon.

Westron wynde when wyll thou blow
the small rayne down can rayne –
Crist yf my love wer in my armys
and I yn my bed agayne!

Enraged by America's war in the Philippines, Twain wrote this prayer in
1905 and sent it to Harper's Bazaar, *which promptly returned it. The*
text was published in 1916, after Twain's death, in Harper's Monthly.

The War Prayer
Mark Twain

Sunday morning came – next day the battalions would leave for the front;
the church was filled; the volunteers were there, their young faces alight with
martial dreams – visions of the stern advance, the gathering momentum, the
rushing charge, the flashing sabers, the flight of the foe, the tumult, the envelop-
ing smoke, the fierce pursuit, the surrender!

Then home from the war, bronzed heroes, welcomed, adored, submerged
in golden seas of glory! With the volunteers sat their dear ones, proud,
happy, and envied by the neighbors and friends who had no sons and broth-
ers to send forth to the field of honor, there to win for the flag, or, failing,
die the noblest of noble deaths. The service proceeded; a war chapter from
the Old Testament was read; the first prayer was said; it was followed by
an organ burst that shook the building, and with one impulse the house
rose, with glowing eyes and beating hearts, and poured out that tremendous
invocation:

> *God the all-terrible! Thou who ordainest,*
> *Thunder thy clarion and lightning thy sword!*

Then came the 'long' prayer. None could remember the like of it for
passionate pleading and moving and beautiful language. The burden of its
supplication was, that an ever-merciful and benignant Father of us all would
watch over our noble young soldiers, and aid, comfort, and encourage them in
their patriotic work; bless them, shield them in the day of battle and the hour
of peril, bear them in His mighty hand, make them strong and confident,

invincible in the bloody onset; help them crush the foe, grant to them and to their flag and country imperishable honor and glory . . .

An aged stranger entered and moved with slow and noiseless step up the main aisle, his eyes fixed upon the minister, his long body clothed in a robe that reached to his feet, his head bare, his white hair descending in a frothy cataract to his shoulders, his seamy face unnaturally pale, pale even to ghastliness. With all eyes following him and wondering, he made his silent way; without pausing, he ascended to the preacher's side and stood there waiting. With shut lids the preacher, unconscious of his presence, continued his moving prayer, and at last finished it with the words, uttered in fervent appeal, 'Bless our arms, grant us the victory, O Lord and God, Father and Protector of our land and flag!'

The stranger touched his arm, motioned him to step aside – which the startled minister did – and took his place. During some moments he surveyed the spellbound audience with solemn eyes, in which burned an uncanny light; then in a deep voice he said:

'I come from the Throne – bearing a message from Almighty God!' The words smote the house with a shock; if the stranger perceived it he gave no attention. 'He has heard the prayer of His servant your shepherd, and will grant it if such be your desire after I, His messenger, shall have explained to you its import – that is to say, its full import. For it is like unto many of the prayers of men, in that it asks for more than he who utters it is aware of – except he pause and think. God's servant and yours has prayed his prayer. Has he paused and taken thought? Is it one prayer? No, it is two – one uttered, and the other not. Both have reached the ear of Him who heareth all supplications, the spoken and the unspoken. Ponder this – keep it in mind. If you would beseech a blessing upon yourself, beware! lest without intent you invoke a curse upon your neighbor at the same time. If you pray for the blessing of rain on your crop which needs it, by that act you are possibly praying for a curse on some neighbor's crop which may not need rain and can be injured by it.

'You have heard your servant's prayer – the uttered part of it. I am commissioned by God to put into words the other part of it – that part which the

138

pastor – and also you in your hearts – fervently prayed silently. And ignorantly and unthinkingly? God grant that it was so! You heard the words 'Grant us the victory, O Lord our God!' That is sufficient. The whole of the uttered prayer is compact into those pregnant words. Elaborations were not necessary. When you have prayed for victory you have prayed for many unmentioned results which follow victory – must follow it, cannot help but follow it. Upon the listening spirit of God fell also the unspoken part of the prayer. He commandeth me to put it into words. Listen!

'Lord our Father, our young patriots, idols of our hearts, go forth into battle – be Thou near them! With them – in spirit – we also go forth from the sweet peace of our beloved firesides to smite the foe. O Lord our God, help us tear their soldiers to bloody shreds with our shells; help us to cover their smiling fields with the pale forms of their patriot dead; help us to drown the thunder of the guns with the shrieks of their wounded, writhing in pain; help us to lay waste their humble homes with a hurricane of fire; help us to wring the hearts of their unoffending widows with unavailing grief; help us to turn them out roofless with their little children to wander unfriended in the wastes of their desolated land in rags and hunger and thirst, sports of the sun flames in summer and the icy winds of winter, broken in spirit, worn with travail, imploring thee for the refuge of the grave and denied it.

'For our sakes who adore Thee, Lord, blast their hopes, blight their lives, protract their bitter pilgrimage, make heavy their steps, water their way with their tears, stain the white snow with the blood of their wounded feet!

'We ask it, in the spirit of love, of Him Who is the Source of Love, and Who is the ever-faithful refuge and friend of all that are sore beset and seek His aid with humble and contrite hearts. Amen.'

(*After a pause.*) 'Ye have prayed it; if ye still desire it, speak! The messenger of the Most High waits.'

Cherokee Traveller's Greeting

I will draw thorns from your feet.
We will walk the White Path of Life together.
Like a brother of my own blood, I will love you.
I will wipe tears from your eyes.
When you are sad, I will put your aching heart to rest.

Mother, Virgin, Goddess

CB

I have a natural sympathy with those who conceive of God as feminine, and in the Christian context with those whose veneration of the divine mother borders on, when it does not actually cross the line into, mariolatry. It is possible that I am extrapolating from my own small life – in which, if I am to be scrupulous, I have to say that I am happier in the company of women, and in which also, to be even more exact, most of what I have learned that has been of value to me I have learned from women.

It seems to me curiously one-sided that all of the giant monotheistic religions are centred on a male God. Some mythographers have read this as an expression of the consolidation in historical time of patriarchal power, founded in war and conquest, and some have argued that it is possible to trace behind the brass and stone of the patriarchy the lineaments of an older mind-set, where God is woman, or at least female. There are shadowy stories, truths half-hinted at: one thinks of Lilith created co-equal with Adam in the suppressed Genesis, replaced by the image of woman as compliant helpmate which has bedevilled relations between men and women ever since.

While compiling this book I was both saddened and puzzled to find so few texts that redress what seems to me an absurd imbalance. I include a number of prayers that are vivid in themselves, but may serve also to point the interested reader to forgotten forests and a lost, perhaps only misplaced, inheritance.

The prayers from the Christian tradition here have, to put it mildly, a troubled relationship with the orthodox view that Mary was a human being chosen as vessel for Christ's incarnation. I have not deliberately chosen heretical or near-heretical texts; I observe simply that few authors, writing in praise of Mary, or addressing her directly, seem capable of staying within bounds. There is some sense in which, for all of these authors, Mary is divine. In the texts I have chosen here woman is seen (and speaks) as that manifestation of the divine likeliest to be constituted in love, despite what is, to my taste, a worrying emphasis on virginity.

The patriarchal God is usually given as judge, lord, stern father, implacable lawgiver: the Other stands open-armed before us.

 CB

Alleluia-Verse for the Virgin
Hildegard of Bingen, trans. Barbara Newman

Alleluia! light
burst from your untouched
womb like a flower
on the farther side
of death. The world-tree
is blossoming. Two
realms become one.

The Queen of Heaven here is Isis, who plays a central role in Apuleius'
The Golden Ass.

O blessed Queen of Heaven . . .
Apuleius

O blessed Queen of Heaven . . . you who make bright all the cities of
the earth with your light of woman, you who nourish all the seeds
of the earth with your warmth, your light changing as the sun moves
near or far: I call upon you by whatever name, in whatever form, seems
right, that you may end my labour and misery, that you may raise up
my faltering hopes and deliver me from that ill-fortune which for so
long has pursued me. Grant peace and rest to me, if it please you, and
freedom from my troubles.

The Milk of Grace

Mechtild of Magdeburg, trans. Brian Pickett

Lady, as you suckled once,
so suckle still
martyrs with strong faith in their hearts,
penitents with holy warnings in their ears,
virgins with your purity,
widows with steadfastness,
oppressors with compassion,
sinners with prayers of repentance.

Lady, you can suckle us still,
for your breasts are still so full –
you cannot restrain them.
Will you then not suckle me,
though your milk may bring you much pain?
For I have seen your breasts so full
that seven streams pour forth all at once from one breast
upon my body and soul.
In that vision you gave me a work to do
which no friend of God can bear without sorrow in the heart.
As you will suckle still until the last day,
so you must be emptied
if God's children and your children are to be weaned
and grow to full, eternal life.
Thereafter, in unbounded pleasure let us know and see the milk
from that same breast which Jesus often kissed.

Contemplating God's Motherhood
Julian of Norwich, trans. Edmund Colledge,
James Walsh and Jean Leclerq

Lord God,
I understand three ways
of contemplating your motherhood.
The first is the foundation
of our nature's creation;
the second is your taking of our nature,
where your motherhood of grace begins;
the third is your motherhood at work.
And in that, by your grace,
everything is penetrated,
in length and in breadth,
in height and in depth,
without end;
and it is all one love.

Ní Dhomhnaill is a gifted contemporary poet in Irish; Montague, a great love poet and one heavily influenced by Graves' theories of the White Goddess, is on home ground translating this homage to the Welsh triple goddess.

Blodewedd
John Montague, after the Irish of Nuala Ní Dhomhnaill

At the least touch of your fingertips
I break into blossom,
my whole chemical composition
transformed.
I sprawl like a grassy meadow,
fragrant in the sun;
at the brush of your palm, all my herbs
and spices spill open

frond by frond, lured to unfold
and exhale in the heat;
wild strawberries rife, and pimpernels
flagrant and scarlet, blushing
down their stems.
To mow that rushy bottom;
sweet scything.

All winter I waited silently
for your appeal.
I withered within, dead to all,
curled away, and deaf as clay,
all my life forces ebbing slowly
till now I come to, at your touch,
revived as from a death swoon.

Your sun lightens my sky
and a wind lifts, like God's angel,
to move the waters;
every inch of me quivers
before your presence,
goose-pimples I get as you glide
over me, and every hair
stands on end.

Hours later I linger
in the ladies toilet,
a sweet scent wafting
from all my pores,
proof positive, if a sign
was needed, that at the least
touch of your fingertips
I break into blossom.

This hymn recapitulates an ancient theme – the divine (or quasi-divine) female as protectress of voyagers. Catholic seafarers have an especial devotion to the first verse and in the right, that is to say the wrong, circumstances never tire of repeating it.

Hail, Queen of Heaven
John Lingard

Hail, Queen of Heaven, the ocean star,
Guide of the wanderer, here below;
Thrown on life's surge, we claim thy care:
Save us from peril and from woe.
Mother of Christ, star of the sea,
Pray for the wanderer, pray for me.

And while to him who reigns above,
In godhead one, in persons three,
The source of life, of grace, of love,
Homage we pay on bended knee,
Virgin most pure, star of the sea,
Pray for the sinner, pray for me.

A relatively late (nineteenth-century) example of the Christian adoption of a pagan antecedent, the goddess of spring; the usual music is from St Basil's Hymnal.

Bring Flowers of the Rarest

Bring flowers of the fairest,
Bring flowers of the rarest,
From garden and woodland
And hillside and vale;
Our full hearts are swelling,
Our glad voices telling
The praise of the loveliest
Rose of the vale.
O Mary, we crown thee
With blossoms today,
Queen of the Angels,
Queen of the May.
O Mary, we crown thee
With blossoms today,
Queen of the Angels,
Queen of the May.

A hymn from the composer of Tosca *and* La Bohème.

Hail, Hail Queen of Heaven
Giacomo Puccini

Hail, hail Queen of Heaven,
Mother of the downhearted,
Star of the divine sea,
Star of the glittering immortal sea.
To every misfortune and grief
You return blessings,
With your gaze
You make holy
All earthly love.

An anonymous verse from fifteenth-century England. 'Our Lorde is the frwte [fruit]' refers to the Tree of Jesse, a lineage tree which traces Christ's ancestry back through David to Jesse. Mary, in this tradition, is assigned a side branch.

Upon My Ryght Syde y Me Leye

Upon my Ryght syde y me leye,
Blesid lady, to thee y pray,
Ffor the teres that ye lete
Upone yowr swete sonnys feete,
Sende me grace for to slepe
And good dremys for to mete,
Slepyng, wakyng, til morowe daye bee.
Our Lorde is the frwte, owre lady is the tree;
Blessid be the blossome that sprange, lady, of the!

Literally:

Upon my right side I me lay,
Blessed lady, to thee I pray,
For the tears that you shed
Upon your sweet son's feet,
Send me grace for to sleep,
And grant I may good dreams meet,
Sleeping, waking, till tomorrow's day be.
Our Lord is the fruit, our lady is the tree;
Blessed be the blossom that sprang, lady, of thee.

Hermann von Reichenau ('Contractus' because he was crippled) was an early eleventh-century Swabian genius, learned in theology, mathematics, astronomy, music and the Latin, Greek and Arabic tongues. He was famed for his monastic virtue and his lovable personality. This prayer is mentioned in Chaucer's 'The Prioress' Tale'.

Alma Redemptoris Mater
Hermann Contractus

Mother of Christ, hear thou thy people's cry,
Star of the deep and Portal of the sky!
Mother of Him who thee from nothing made.
Sinking we strive and call to thee for aid:
Oh, by what joy which Gabriel brought to thee,
Thou Virgin first and last, let us thy mercy see.

A thirteenth-century hymn, attributed to Pope Innocent III (d. 1216), St Bonaventure or, most commonly, Jacopone da Todi (1230–1306).

Stabat Mater Dolorosa
trans. Fr Edward Caswall

At the Cross, her station keeping,
stood the mournful Mother weeping,
close to Jesus to the last.

Through her heart, His sorrow sharing,
all his bitter anguish bearing,
now at length the sword has passed.

O how sad and sore distressed
was that Mother, highly blest,
of the sole-begotten One.

Christ above in torment hangs,
she beneath beholds the pangs,
of her dying glorious son.

Is there one who would not weep,
whelmed in miseries so deep,
Christ's dear Mother to behold?

Can the human heart refrain
from partaking in her pain,
in that Mother's pain untold?

Bruised, derided, cursed, defiled,
she beheld her tender Child
all with scourges rent:

For the sins of His own nation,
saw Him hang in desolation
Till His spirit forth He sent.

O thou Mother! fount of love!
Touch my spirit from above,
make my heart with thine accord:

Make me feel as thou hast felt;
make my soul to glow and melt
with the love of Christ my Lord.

Holy Mother! pierce me through,
in my heart each wound renew
of my Saviour crucified:

Let me share with thee His pain,
who for all my sins was slain,
who for me in torments died.

Let me mingle tears with thee,
Mourning Him who mourned for me,
all the days that I might live:

By the Cross with thee to stay,
there with thee to weep and pray,
is all I ask of thee to give.

Virgin of all virgins blest!
Listen to my fond request:
let me share thy grief divine;

Let me, to my latest breath,
in my body bear the death
of that dying Son of thine.

Wounded with His every wound,
steep my soul till it hath swooned
in His very Blood away.

Be to me, O Virgin, nigh,
lest in flames I burn and die,
in His awful Judgement Day.

Christ, when Thou shall call me hence,
be Thy Mother my defence,
be Thy Cross my victory;

While my body here decays,
may my soul Thy goodness praise,
safe in paradise with Thee. Amen.

It was a new and pagan dawn . . .
Michael Hartnett

It was a new and pagan dawn
and gods in quiet museums
turned their antique eyes to the snow
around Piraeus.
And electric Zeus
roared ice, and Pan danced,
and the old music of the old gods
trilled marble octaves through the Athens streets,
and the cypress woke,
sombre on the Acropolis,
and the Attic hills
rushed inland, their wake
an undulating whirl
of starlings and white smoke,
and the cypress sang.

White waists of women
were the frantic trees,
and branches, human
immaculate hands;
and there was a river laughter
and a wild talking in tree-groves
and strange voices by deserted pools.
Came ashore, her shell an Italian ship,
her foam the spring snow, an Aphrodite;
and the bees to the honey that came from
the sea, pointed their strange directive dance.
Cypress-slender on the Acropolis

she walked, through the rows of welcoming gods,
quiet; her hair side-tressed to show one ear,
so white, a marble immobile beauty,
still as the untenanted Parthenon.

The Muses invoked here are daughters of Pieria, a Macedonian province home to Orpheus and site of Mount Olympus.

Resplendent daughters . . .
Solon

Resplendent daughters of memory and Olympian Zeus, Pierian Muses, hearken to my prayer. Grant that I have prosperity from the blessed gods and a good reputation always from all men; grant that in these circumstances I be sweet to my friends and bitter to my enemies, viewed with respect by the former and with dread by the latter.

I long to have money, but I am unwilling to possess it unjustly, for retribution assuredly comes afterwards. Wealth which the gods give remains with a man, secure from the lowest foundation to the top, whereas wealth which men honour with violence comes in disorder, an unwilling attendant persuaded by unjust actions, and it is quickly mixed with ruin.

Brigit, or Brigid or Bríd, was a classical Celtic triple goddess associated with wisdom, poetry and philosophy, high places, leaping flames and enduring wells. Christianized and carried into the folk tradition, she is the saint of the hearth and the homeplace, an unfailing protectress.

Blessing of Brigit

Each day and each night
That I say the Descent of Brigit

I shall not be slain,
I shall not be sworded,
I shall not be put in cell,
I shall not be hewn,
I shall not be riven,
I shall not be anguished,
I shall not be wounded,
I shall not be ravaged,
I shall not be blinded,
I shall not be made naked,
I shall not be left bare.
Nor will Christ
Leave me forgotten.

Nor fire shall burn me,
Nor sun shall burn me,
Nor moon shall blanch me.

Nor water shall drown me,
Nor flood shall drown me,
Nor brine shall drown me.

Nor seed of fairy host shall lift me,
Nor seed of airy host shall lift me,
Nor earthly being destroy me.

I am under the shielding
Of good Brigit each day;
I am under the shielding
Of good Brigit each night.

I am under the keeping
Of the Nurse of Mary,
Each early and late,
Every dark, every light.

Brigit is my comrade-woman,
Brigit is my maker of song,
Brigit is my helping-woman,
My choicest of women, my guide.

Death and Fear

C&

Sogyal Rinpoche, addressing a large audience in a Dublin hotel, once posed the question: 'What's all this fuss about dying?' He went on: 'What's the big deal? You breathe in, you breathe out, you breathe in, you breathe out – and then you don't breathe in again. Simple. It's not difficult. Anyone can do it.' Rinpoche has a gift for constructive mischief, and his point on that occasion, as I understood it at the time, was to dislocate his audience's preoccupation with the abstract idea of death – disabling in its immensity – and to draw our attention to the small act of dying, which requires no more of us than ceasing to breathe.

In all revelation-based religions there are core propositions about death. The god of life is also the god of death; how we live life here will affect how (or even if) we will live life in death; the god who teaches us how to live also instructs us on the afterlife. So, we pray to God or to the gods that we may be saved, that we may be spared purgatory or hell, that we may be reunited with those who have gone before, be present for those who will follow after. We pray for the forgiveness of those sins which may stand between us and everlasting bliss, we pray for support in the living of this life that we be not excluded from the joys of the next. We also, of course, pray in the strong confidence that the next life is guaranteed by the same god who guarantees this life, and in the same way.

The prayers in the first part of this chapter are founded in the widespread belief that God will sustain us in this afterlife, that dying is transition, a passage from this life into the next. The alert reader will find the salt of all-too-human doubt in some of these prayers, a whistling past the graveyard that in my view neither adds to nor subtracts from their power as prayers.

Sifting through my notes for this book, I found myself coming back, time and again, to a selection of Sepulchral Epigrams I had copied down from the *Greek Anthology*. For a long time I resisted the idea that these had anything to do with this collection – it's a common enough experience, extraneous material elbowing its way into a book in progress – until eventually it dawned on me that these texts, and a handful of others included here as examples drawn from a wider field, are indeed prayers, but prayers in the absence of God. They work for me as prayers because when I say the words over to myself I am overtaken by a sense of how beautiful this life is, how awesome and irrevocable the fact of death is, but above all because I find in the words a profound and consoling sense of human dignity. Prayers in the face of God have this in common with the prayers of unbelief: that they are addressed to the living, give words to the living with which they may orient or console themselves. These texts arrange and prepare my consciousness in the same way as conventional prayers did when I was much younger, and a believer. They open out the starry dimensions. They open out my understanding heart.

For those who cannot accept death, for whom grief is endless, those incapable of being reconciled to loss, there is perhaps the consolation of stoic beauty in Edna St Vincent Millay's 'Dirge without Music'. As in Stevenson's crisp and dignified eight-line 'Requiem', these are hymns to life in the face of inescapable death.

⍥

E Tenebris
Oscar Wilde

Come down, O Christ, and help me! reach thy hand,
For I am drowning in a stormier sea
Than Simon on thy lake of Galilee:
The wine of life is spilt upon the sand,
My heart is in some famine-murdered land
Whence all good things have perished utterly.
And well I know my soul in hell must lie
If I this night before God's throne should stand.
'He sleeps perchance, or rideth to the chase,
Like Baal, when his prophets howled that name
From morn to noon on Carmel's smitten height.'
Nay, peace, I shall behold, before the night,
The feet of brass, the robe more white than flame,
The wounded hands, the weary human face.

Tie the Strings to My Life, My Lord . . .
Emily Dickinson

Tie the strings to my life, my Lord,
    Then I am ready to go!
Just a look at the horses –
    Rapid! That will do!

Put me in on the firmest side,
    So I shall never fall;
For we must ride to the Judgment,
    And it's partly down hill.

But never I mind the bridges
    And never I mind the sea;
Held fast in everlasting race
    By my own choice and thee.

Good-by to the life I used to live,
    And the world I used to know;
And kiss the hills for me, just once;
    Now I am ready to go!

A Prayer for Grace
Robert Louis Stevenson

Grant that we here before Thee may be set free from the fear of vicis-situde and the fear of death, may finish what remains before us of our course without dishonour to ourselves or hurt to others, and, when the day comes, may die in peace. Deliver us from fear and favour: from mean hopes and cheap pleasures. Have mercy on each in his deficiency; let him be not cast down; support the stumbling on the way, and give at last rest to the weary.

Written down by Aubrey in 1686, this song from Yorkshire is clearly far older. The idea of purgatorial pilgrimage, where salvation depends on good deeds done in this life, goes to the roots of Indo-European culture. Some musicologists think the air to which the words are sung goes back to Old Norse, perhaps even beyond that.

A Lyke-Wake Dirge

This ae nighte, this ae nighte,
– *Every nighte and alle,*
Fire and fleet and candle-lighte
      And Christe receive thy saule.

When thou from hence away are past
– *Every nighte and alle,*
To Whinny-muir thou com'st at last
And Christ receive thy saule.

If ever thou gavest hosen and shoon,
– *Every nighte and alle,*
Sit thee down and put them on;
And Christ receive thy saule.

If hosen and shoon thou ne'er gav'st nane
– *Every nighte and alle,*
The whinnes sall prick thee to the bare bane;
And Christ receive thy saule.

From Whinny-muir when thou may'st pass,
– *Every nighte and alle,*
To Brig o' Dread thou com'st at last
And Christ receive thy saule.

From Brig o' Dread when thou may'st pass,
– *Every nighte and alle,*
To Purgatory fire thou com'st at last;
And Christ receive thy saule.

If ever thou gavest meat or drink,
– *Every nighte and alle,*
The fire sall never make thee shrink;
And Christ receive thy saule.

If meat or drink thou ne'er gav'st nane,
– *Every nighte and alle,*
The fire will burn thee to the bare bane;
And Christ receive thy saule.

This ae nighte, this ae nighte,
– *Every nighte and alle,*
Fire and fleet and candle-lighte
        And Christe receive thy saule.

Three wishes I ask . . .

Three wishes I ask of the King when I part from my body: May I have nothing to confess, may I have no enemy, may I own nothing!

Three wishes I ask this day of the King, ruler of suns: May I have no dignity or honours that may lead me into torment! May I not work without reward before the Christ of this world! May God take my soul when it is most pure!

Finally, may I not be guilty when my three wishes have been spoken!

Myers was the founder of the Society for Psychical Research and an early Theosophist. His Human Personality and Its Survival of Bodily Death *was published posthumously.*

A Last Appeal
Frederick William Henry Myers

O somewhere, somewhere, God unknown,
Exist and be!
I am dying; I am all alone,
I must have Thee!

God! God! my sense, my soul, my all,
Dies in the cry:
Saw'st thou the faint star flame and fall?
Ah! it was I.

I Am the World
Dora Sigerson Shorter

I am the song, that rests upon the cloud;
I am the sun;
I am the dawn, the day, the hiding shroud,
When dusk is done.

I am the changing colours of the tree;
The flower uncurled;
I am the melancholy of the sea;
I am the world.

The other souls that, passing in their place,
Each in his groove;
Outstretching hands that chain me and embrace,
Speak and reprove.

'O atom of that law, by which the earth
Is poised and whirled;
Behold! you hurrying with the crowd assert
You are the world.'

Am I not one with all the things that be
Warm in the sun?
All that my ears can hear, or eyes can see,
Till all be done.

Of song and shine, of changing leaf apart,
Of bud uncurled;
With all the sense pulsing at my heart,
I am the world.

One day the song that drifts upon the wind
I shall not hear:
Nor shall the rosy shoots to eyes grown blind
Again appear.

Deaf, in the dark, I shall arise and throw
From off my soul
The withered world with all its joy and woe,
That was my goal.

I shall arise, and like a shooting star
Slip from my place;
So lingering see the old world from afar
Revolve in space.

And know more things than all the wise may know
Till all be done;
Till One shall come who, breathing on the stars,
Blows out the sun.

An Inca's Death Prayer

O Creator of men,
your servant speaks.
Look on him now,
King of Cuzco.

Do not forget me,
Noble Creator,
You of my dreams.
Will you forget,
And I on the point of death?
Wilt you ignore my prayer,
Or will you make known
Who you are?
You may be what I thought –
Or you may be a phantom,
A thing to cause fear.
If only I knew!
If only it could be revealed!
You, who made me out of earth,
You, who fashioned me out of clay,
Look now upon me!
Creator, who are you truly?
I am very old.

Often considered the very model of a Victorian Anglican, Tennyson was in fact a pantheist, a fact confirmed by his son after the laureate's death. In his great work In Memoriam *Tennyson writes: 'There lives more faith in honest doubt, believe me, than in half the creeds.'*

Crossing the Bar
Alfred Lord Tennyson

Sunset and evening star,
And one clear call for me!
And may there be no moaning of the bar,
When I put out to sea,

But such a tide as moving seems asleep,
Too full for sound and foam,
When that which drew from out the boundless deep
Turns again home.

Twilight and evening bell,
And after that the dark!
And may there be no sadness or farewell,
When I embark;

For tho' from out our bourne of Time and Place
The flood may bear me far,
I hope to see my Pilot face to face
When I have crost the bar.

Campion's rather orthodox religious ideas achieve a lyric grace and occasional strangeness when set, as most of his words were, to music, often his own.

View me, Lord, a work of thine . . .
Thomas Campion

View me, Lord, a work of thine:
Shall I then lie drown'd in night?
Might thy grace in me but shine,
I should seem made all of light.

But my soul still surfeits so
On the poisoned baits of sin,
That I strange and ugly grow,
All is dark and foul within.

Cleanse me, Lord, that I may kneel
At thine altar, pure and white:
They that once thy mercies feel,
Gaze no more on earth's delight.

Worldly joys like shadows fade,
When the heav'nly light appears;
But the cov'nants thou hast made,
Endless, know nor days, nor years.

In thy word, Lord, is my trust,
To thy mercies fast I fly.
Though I am but clay and dust,
Yet thy grace can lift me high.

Never weather-beaten sail . . .
Thomas Campion

Never weather-beaten sail more willing bent to shore,
Never tired pilgrim's limbs affected slumber more,
Than my wearied sprite now longs to fly out of my troubled breast.
O come quickly, sweetest Lord, and take my soul to rest.
Ever-blooming are the joys of heav'ns high paradise,
Cold age deafs not there our ears, nor vapour dims our eyes;
Glory there the sun outshines, whose beams the blessed only see;
O come quickly, glorious Lord, and raise my sprite to thee.

A hymn that rehearses the author's reluctance to accept an invitation from King James I to go as chaplain on a military expedition to Germany. Born a Catholic, Donne converted to the Anglican church and finished his days as Dean of St Paul's, London.

A Hymne to Christ, at the Author's Last Going into Germany
John Donne

In what torne ship soever I embarke,
That ship shall be the embleme of thy Arke;
What sea soever swallow mee, that flood
Shall be to mee an embleme of thy blood;
Though thou with clouds of anger do disguise
Thy face; yet through that maske I know those eyes,
     Which, though they turn away sometimes,
     They never will despise.

I sacrifice this Iland unto thee,
And all whom I lov'd there, and who lov'd mee;
When I have put our seas twixt them and mee,
Put thou thy sea twix betwixt my sinnes and thee.
As the trees sap doth seeke the root below
In winter, in my winter now I goe,
     Where none but thee, th'Eternall root
     Of true love I may know.

Nor thou nor thy religion dost controule,
The amorousness of an harmonious soule,
But thou woulds't have that love thy selfe: as thou
Art jealous, Lord, so I am jealous now,

That lov'st not, till from loving more, thou free
My soule: who ever gives takes libertie:
      O, if thou car'st not whom I love,
      Alas thou lov'st not mee.

Seale then this bill of my Divorce to All,
On whom those fainter beames of love did fall;
Marry those loves, which in youth scattered bee
On Fame, Wit, Hopes (false mistresses), to thee.
Churches are best for Prayer, that have least light:
To see God only, I goe out of sight:
      And to scape stormy days, I chuse
      An Everlasting night.

Death, Be Not Proud
John Donne

Death, be not proud, though some have called thee
Mighty and dreadful, for thou are not so;
For those whom thou think'st thou dost overthrow
Die not, poor Death; nor yet can't thou kill me.
From rest and sleep, which but thy picture be,
Much pleasure; then from thee much more must flow;
And soonest our best men with thee do go –
Rest of their bones and souls' delivery!
Thou'rt slave to fate, chance, kings and desperate men,
And dost with poison, war, and sickness dwell;
And poppy or charms can make us sleep as well
And better than thy stroke. Why swell'st thou then?
One short sleep past, we wake eternally,
And Death shall be no more: Death, thou shalt die.

This Southern Bushman tale was published in Markowitz's The Rebirth of the Ostrich, *Gaborone, Botswana, 1971.*

The Day We Die
trans. Arthur Markowitz

The day we die
the wind comes down
to take away
our footprints.

The wind makes dust
to cover up
the marks we left
while walking.

For otherwise
the thing would seem
as if we were
still living.

Therefore the wind
is he who comes
to blow away
our footprints.

Dirge without Music
Edna St Vincent Millay

I am not resigned to the shutting away of loving hearts in the hard ground.
So it is, and so it will be, for so it has been, time out of mind:
Into the darkness they go, the wise and the lovely. Crowned
With lilies and with laurel they go; but I am not resigned.

Lovers and thinkers, into the earth with you.
Be one with the dull, the indiscriminate dust.
A fragment of what you felt, of what you knew,
A formula, a phrase remains, but the best is lost.

The answers quick and keen, the honest look, the laughter, the love,
They are gone. They are gone to feed the roses. Elegant and curled
Is the blossom. Fragrant is the blossom. I know. But I do not approve.
More precious was the light in your eyes than all the roses in the world.

Down, down, down into the darkness of the grave
Gently they go, the beautiful, the tender, the kind;
Quietly they go, the intelligent, the witty, the brave.
I know. But I do not approve. And I am not resigned.

Letters to the Dead: Funeral Scroll
Diana O'Hehir

Some of the handsome illustrations of the Scribe Anis' papyrus show him making the Underworld journey accompanied by his wife, who was still alive

Greetings to my husband and brother.
Tell me, friend whom I miss, what I have done to anger you.
I was a careful wife,
Boiled herbs for your sickness, knelt by your funeral bier.
In childhood we swam in the pool; you watched; the damp cloth clung to
*   my breasts.*
Please give me silence now.
Let me sleep.
Come by my bed tonight in a dream.

The funeral was gray, green and black on a tan ground;
She followed the cart, bent over, elbows awkward,
The mummy watching through its white mask.

The Scribe, tan and white on a burnt-umber ground,
Has arrived safely past the dangers of the boat, the crocodile, the
    Worm with the striped head.

He says, 'The tusks are split by an iron harpoon.'
He says, 'I've come from the pool of fire.'
His wife is not present in these pictures.

Brother, I've ordered a new funeral scroll, black with red titles, the deco-
*   rations in malachite and lapis.*

The Scribe will draw me into these scenes.
Is the West treating you as it should?

I ask again
To see you in a dream.

Now she appears in the Underworld beside a blue river;
She walks through V-shaped waves, three steps behind him.
'If it breathes air, I will breathe air,' she says.

The jackal-headed god leads her
By his thin hand.
After this she is in many pictures.
She worships a green-skinned god, admires a table of shens-cakes,
Wears a wig, necklace and bracelets,
Holds an emblem of pleasure.

Husband, I am reading your scroll
Where I walk behind you towards the Kingdom of Rushes.
Those events aren't over for you; you're still
Crossing the Waterfowl Lake, the Turquoise Stream, the Eastern Gate of
the Sky;
One of your days is a thousand
Of our years.

Brother,
Please.
I wake each morning before the geese.

One might read a fear of Norse invaders in this tale from Western Scotland, but the dread seems more universal and primitive. Strong enough, in any case, to prompt the reciter to pray for delivery. The prayer is in the silence after.

The Cats Are Come on Us
from the Carmina Gadelica

The Cats are come on us,
The Cats are come on us,
The Cats are come on us,
The Cats are come on us,
    They are come on us.

To break in upon us,
To lift the spoil from us,
To steal the kine from us,
To cudgel our horses,
To strip bare our houses,
    They are come on us.

They are come, they are come,
They are come, they are come,
They are come, they are come,
They are come in the ill hour,
    They are found amidst us.

The Cats are come, Cats are come,
The Cats are come, Cats are come,
The Cats are come, Cats are come,
The Cats are come in the evil hour,
    Their stroke is upon us.

The children of wicked men
In storm and in wind
Are in the heathery hollows
Their blood on the field,
Their shafts by their sides,
      And their quivers well filled.

The Cats are come on us,
The Cats are come on us,
The Cats are come on us,
The Cats are come on us,
      They are come upon us.

For murder and for mauling
They are come,
For howling and for hazard
They are come,
For pillage and for plunder,
In rain and in wind,
To lift the calving kine
      They are come upon us.

The cats are come,
The cats are come,
The cats are come,
The cats are come,
Cats are come on us,
The Cats are come in the evil hour,
      Their stroke is upon us.

To drive the calving kine,
To lift away the sheep,
For blood and for wrath,
For weeping and for wailing,
For blood and for wrath,
Marching on Thursday,
    They are come upon us.

A Selection of Sepulchral Epigrams
from The Greek Anthology

223 – Thyillus

The castanet dancer Aristion who used to toss her hair among the pines in honour of Cybele, carried away by the music of the horned flute; she who could empty one upon the other three cups of untempered wine, rests here beneath the poplars, no more taking delight in love and the fatigue of the night-festivals. A long farewell to revels and frenzy! It lies low, the holy head that was covered erst by garlands of flowers.

264 – Leonidas

A good voyage to all who travel on the sea; but let him who looses his cable from my tomb, if the storm carries him like me to the haven of Hades, blame not the inhospitable deep, but his own daring.

269 – Plato

Mariners, may ye be safe on sea and land; but know that this tomb ye are passing is a shipwrecked man's.

276 – Hegesippus

The fishermen brought up from the sea in their net a half-eaten man, a most mournful relic of some sea-voyage. They sought not for unholy gain, but him and the fishes too they buried under this light coat of sand. Thou hast, O land, the whole of the shipwrecked man, but instead of the rest of his flesh thou hast the fishes who fed on it.

277 – Callimachus

Who art thou, shipwrecked stranger? Leontichus found thee here dead on the beach, and buried thee in this tomb, weeping for his own uncertain life; for he also rests not, but travels over the sea like a gull.

278 – Archias of Byzantium

Not even now I am dead shall I, shipwrecked Theris, cast up on land by the waves, forget the sleepless surges. For here under the brine-beaten hill, near the sea my foe, a stranger made my grave; and, ever wretched that I am, even among the dead the hateful roar of the billows sounds in my ears. Not even Hades gave me rest from trouble, since I alone even in death cannot lie in unbroken repose.

282 – Theodoridas

I am the tomb of a shipwrecked man; but set sail, stranger; for when we were lost, the other ships voyaged on.

288 – Antipater

I belong entirely to neither now I am dead, but sea and land possess an equal portion of me. My flesh the fishes ate in the sea, but my bones have been washed up on this cold beach.

293 – Isidorus of Aegae

No tempest, no stormy setting of a constellation overwhelmed Nicophemus in the waters of the Libyan Sea. But alas, unhappy man! stayed by a calm he was burnt up by thirst. This too was the work of the winds. Ah, what a curse they are to sailors, whether they blow or be silent!

Theris, the old man who got his living from his lucky weels, who rode on the sea more than a gull, the preyer on fishes, the seine-hauler, the prober of crevices in the rocks, who sailed on no many-oared ship, in spite of all owed not his end to Arcturus, nor did any tempest drive to death his many decades, but he died in his reed hut, going out like a lamp of his own accord owing to his length of years. This tomb was set up not by his children or wife, but by the guild of his fellow fishermen.

('. . . to Arcturus': i.e. not to the equinoctial gales, coming as they do in September, the season of Arcturus' setting)

349 – Anonymous

After eating little and drinking little and suffering much sickness I lasted long, but at length I did die. A curse on you all!

350 – Anonymous

Ask not, sea-farer, whose tomb I am, but thyself chance upon a kinder sea.

Requiem

Robert Louis Stevenson

Under the wide and starry sky
Dig the grave and let me lie:
Glad did I live and gladly die,
And I laid me down with a will.

This be the verse you 'grave for me:
Here he lies where he long'd to be;
Home is the sailor, home from the sea,
And the hunter home from the hill.

A Note of Thanks

I am very grateful to the Library, Trinity College, Dublin, and to its staff, for the courteous and skilled assistance afforded me in my researches. I owe a particular debt of thanks to the following: Iris Bedford, Admissions Supervisor; Brian O'Connell, Subject Librarian, Religions and Philosophy; Denis McKennedy, Supervisor of Santry Book Repository; Leah Malcolm and, especially, Philip Bedford, Library assistants. I am also grateful to Professor Terence Brown, for smoothing my way.

My editor, Brendan Barrington, was a model of helpfulness and good-humoured patience as always – and well he might be, as it was he who enticed me to this labour of Sisyphus in the first place. I like to think he didn't know what he was getting me into, but when I finally emerged from the dust clouds he was there with his shaping intelligence to come to the aid of a slightly bewildered party.

Colm Tóibín came up with the title, and hence the idea, of this book, and planted it in Mr Barrington's mind. I am grateful to Colm for, all unknowingly and at a remove, sending me down a path I might not otherwise have travelled.

I am grateful to all those who facilitated the granting of permissions to include in this book work for which they hold the copyrights.

Finally, I am grateful to Paula Meehan, for her loving forbearance when I got cranky and for her many shrewd suggestions as I struggled to put order on an intractable mass of material.

I dedicate this book to my philosophy teachers Garrett Barden and Brendan O'Mahony OFM, who were kind to me when I was very young.

Benignitas lumen perennis est,
nec unquam obliviscar

ॐ

Acknowledgements

ભ

We are grateful for permission to republish copyright material contained in this collection as follows:

ALCUIN OF YORK (attrib.): 'He lay with quiet heart in the stern', Helen Waddell (trans.), from *More Latin Lyrics*, Dame Felicitas Corrigan OSB (ed.) (Victor Gollancz, 1976), reprinted by permission of the estate of the translator.

BLACK ELK: 'Grandfather, Great Spirit' from *Black Elk Speaks: Being the Life Story of a Holy Man of the Oglala Sioux*, Black Elk and John G. Neihardt, by permission of the University of Nebraska Press. © 1932, 1959, 1972 John G. Neihardt. © 1961 the John G. Neihardt Trust. © 2000 the University of Nebraska Press. Reprinted by permission of the publisher.

GAVIN CHAPPELL: 'The Nine Herbs Charm', reprinted by permission of the author.

RANDALL D. CHESNUTT: 'Prayer of a Convert to Judaism' (trans.), reprinted by permission of the translator.

EMILY DICKINSON: 'Tie the Strings to My Life, Lord' and 'Exultation', reprinted by permission of the publishers and the Trustees of Amherst College from the *The Poems of Emily Dickinson: Variorum Edition*, Ralph W. Franklin, ed., (The Belkaap Press of Harvard University Press), © 1998 by the President and Fellows of Harvard College.

CAROL ANN DUFFY: 'Prayer' from *Mean Time* (Anvil Press Poetry, 1993), reprinted by permission of the publisher.

and 'Be careful, o man', Paul Jackson SJ (trans.), from *The Hundred Letters* (Paulist Press, 1980), reprinted by permission of the publisher.

MECHTILD OF MAGDEBURG: 'The Milk of Grace', trans. Brian Pickett, from *The Heart of Love* (St Paul Publications, 1991), reprinted by permission of the translator; 'O Lord, love me intensely', Oliver Davies (trans.), from *Beguine Spirituality: An Anthology*, Fiona Bowie (ed.) (SPCK, 2002), reprinted by permission of the publisher.

JOHN MONTAGUE: 'Blodewedd', reprinted by permission of the translator.

SIR HENRY NEWBOLT: 'The Final Mystery', permission granted by Mr Peter Newbolt.

DIANA O'HEHIR: 'Letters to the Dead: Funeral Scroll' and 'Spell for Protecting the Heart after Death' from *Spells for Not Dying Again* (Eastern Washington University Press, 1996), reprinted by permission of the publisher.

RICHARD PACKHAM: 'Atheist Prayer', reprinted by permission of the author.

MARGUERITE PORETE: 'Here Speaks Love' from *Mediaeval Women Writers*, Katharina M. Wilson (ed.) (University of Georgia Press, 1984), reprinted by permission of the publisher.

ROBIN SKELTON: 'Death Rite of the Gabon Pygmies' and 'Journey Charm' from *Spellcraft* (McClelland & Stewart, 1978), reprinted by permission of the publisher.

GARY SNYDER: 'A Turning Verse for the Billions of Beings' from *Danger on Peaks* (Shoemaker & Hoard, 2005), reprinted by permission of the publisher; 'Prayer for the Great Family' from *Turtle Island* (New Directions Publishing Corporation, 1974), reprinted by permission of the publisher.

ELIZABETH STAEGLIN OF TÖSS: 'Uplifted in God', trans. Brian Pickett, from *The Heart of Love* (St Paul Publications, 1991), reprinted by permission of the translator.

EDMOND BORDEAUX SZEKELY: 'God Speaks to Man' from *The Essene Gospel of Peace* (trans.), reprinted by permission of Ms Deborah Szekely.

James H. Charlesworth (ed.), J. J. Collins (trans.), *The Old Testament Pseudepigrapha*, vol. 1 (Doubleday, 1983, copyright James H. Charlesworth): 'The Battle of the Stars', 'Against the Pride of Kings', 'Eschatological Prophecy', 'Fragment Two', 'Fragmentary Oracle' and 'A Riddle on the Name of God', reprinted by permission of Random House, Inc., and Darton, Longman and Todd.

Oliver Davies (trans. & introduction), with Thomas O'Loughlin, *Celtic Spirituality* (Paulist Press, 2000): 'The First Word I Say', 'The Breastplate of Laidcenn', 'Hymn at the Lighting of the Paschal Candle', 'On the Flightiness of Thought' and 'All alone in my little cell', reprinted by permission of the publisher.

Kenneth Hurlstone Jackson (ed. & trans.), *A Celtic Miscellany* (Penguin Classics, 1972), 'A Charm with Yarrow' and 'The Wish of Manchán of Liath', reprinted by permission of Thomson Publishing Services on behalf of Taylor & Francis.

T.J. Knab (ed.), *A Scattering of Jades* (University of Arizona Press, 2003): 'Our Lord' and 'Be Indomitable, O My Heart', reprinted by permission of the publisher. Nahuatl translations © Rita Wilensky 1984.